ESPECIALLY FOR

Sherry

FROM

Bob Jim & Kids

DATE
"50"

Happy Birthday

god bless you ..

WHISPERS OF WISDOM FOR WOMEN

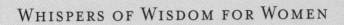

WHISPERS OF WISDOM FOR WOMEN

More Than 100 Gentle, Encouraging Meditations

BARBOUR
PUBLISHING

© 2012 by Barbour Publishing, Inc.

ISBN 978-1-61626-668-4

Cover and interior design: Kirk DouPonce, DogEared Design

Published by Barbour Publishing, Inc., P.O. Box 719, Uhrichsville, Ohio 44683
www.barbourbooks.com

Our mission is to publish and distribute inspirational products offering exceptional value and biblical encouragement to the masses.

 Member of the
Evangelical Christian
Publishers Association

Printed in India.

INTRODUCTION

God wants us to live wise lives, so He shares His wisdom with us through His Word. When we live according to God's principles, we read and hear whispers of wisdom every day—as we read a devotion, study the Bible, listen to biblical teaching, or enjoy Christian music that is grounded in His truths. We need to be surrounded by the truths He has shared with us.

Without God's wisdom, our lives would be chaos. As we faced troubles, we'd be stymied about how to handle them. Though we'd try to make good choices, we'd find ourselves inadvertently in trouble. Though we'd want to do good, we'd hardly know what direction to go in.

God's Word has the answer for everything we experience in our lives, every day. No challenge is too great for Him, and none is too small. He's there for us, whether our lives are joyous or sad.

Drink in God's Word daily through the devotional readings of *Whispers of Wisdom for Women*, which are all based on His wisdom. Make them a part of your life, and be blessed.

RUN HOME

"Don't be afraid, I've redeemed you. I've called your name. You're mine."

ISAIAH 43:1 MSG

Remember when you were a child and you ran outside to play? When it came time for dinner, your mom called you in. She called you by name. And you stopped whatever you were doing and ran. You ran home.

Now you're all grown up. And there is still one who protects you, provides for you, and nourishes you. It's God, the One who got you started. He calls you by your name. You are His! He longs for you to run home to Him!

Listen! Be still. Quiet your thoughts. Do you hear Him? He's calling your name!

Drop whatever you're doing and run! Run into His arms. Allow Him to fill you with His Spirit and peace. Allow Him to love you with an everlasting love. Allow Him to feed you on His Word. Allow Him to hold you tight. He will never let you fall, never let you go. You need not be afraid. You're home!

DONNA K. MALTESE

Lord, I hear You calling my name!
Here I am, Lord! Here I am! I'm coming home!

It is a great thing to enter the inner chamber,
and shut the door, and meet the Father in secret.
It is a greater thing to open the door again,
and go out, in an enjoyment of that presence
which nothing can disturb.

ANDREW MURRAY

RECEIVING GOD'S EMBRACE

*See what great love the Father has lavished on us,
that we should be called children of God! And that is what we are!*

1 JOHN 3:1 NIV

Some people are born "huggers." They greet family members or complete strangers in the same way. They just can't help themselves. They must lavish love on those around them. Most of us would agree that the closer the relationship, the more meaningful the hug.

Can you imagine receiving an embrace from our heavenly Father, the God of the universe? God lavished His love on us when He sent Jesus to earth. Jesus' sacrificial death on our behalf paved the way for adoption into God's family by faith. When we receive the gift of Jesus, we become children of God. We are no longer strangers, alienated from a holy God. We have become family!

As you ponder God's great love for you, picture Jesus hanging on the cross. With arms outstretched, He came to embrace you! Receive the embrace of your heavenly Father today!

JULIE RAYBURN

Dear Lord, I need Your embrace.
May I receive the abundant love You desire to lavish upon me
because I am Your child.

Wherever you are spiritually,
whatever you have been through emotionally,
you are already wrapped in the Lord's embrace.
Held by nail-scarred hands.
Enfolded in the arms of One who believes in you,
supports you, treasures you, and loves you.

LIZ CURTIS HIGGS

A Request for Wisdom

"Now, O LORD my God, you have made me king instead of my father, David, but I am like a little child who doesn't know his way around."

1 KINGS 3:7 NLT

After Solomon has replaced David as the king of Israel, God appears to Solomon in a dream and offers to give him whatever he wants. Instead of asking for wealth or long life or triumph over his enemies, Solomon asks for wisdom. Solomon wants to rule wisely, but he feels like a little child. Therefore, Solomon asks for the ability to decide between right and wrong and to lead his people as a true follower of God.

Solomon's example stands out for us today. We need wisdom in our relationships.

Perhaps you have felt like a little child. A new situation arises, an argument you've never had before, a life-altering change, the death of a loved one. God is waiting for your prayer, and He desires to guide you in His unsurpassed wisdom. Like little children, we must ask God for help; He will help us find our way.

MANDY NYDEGGER

Dear Lord,
You are wise beyond understanding.
Grant me Your wisdom today in my relationships.

Wisdom is repeatedly personified as a woman in the
book of Proverbs. That's certainly by design.
Wisdom isn't pictured as a testosterone-loaded taxi driver.
It doesn't ignore us and drive by as we wave, or finally
stop and shove us helplessly into the backseat and race
us to an unknown destination. Wisdom is pictured as
a woman who uses truthful, caring words—
words that call, guide, encourage, and direct us
as we learn to "walk in wisdom."

JOHN TRENT

GIRLS' DAY OUT

*Be friendly with everyone. Don't be proud and feel that you are
smarter than others. Make friends with ordinary people.*

ROMANS 12:16 CEV

Sometimes you just need a good girls' day out. It's nice
to hang out with a husband or boyfriend, but sometimes
it is also important just to spend time with the girls.

A good girlfriend can come from many places.
Maybe she's a coworker who likes to have lunch but
whom you don't see outside the office. Perhaps she's
a church friend. Maybe she's your sister or someone
you've known since you sat next to each other on the
kindergarten mat. Spending time with other women
can be refreshing. They can provide support and
understanding in a way to which a member of the
opposite sex may not always be able to relate.

When you find a good girlfriend, cherish
her. Make time for calls and visits and let
her know that you love being her sister in
Christ.

CHRISTAN M. THOMAS

God, thank You for giving me good girlfriends.
Help me to be a sister in Christ with each and every one of my
friends and to spend time cultivating our relationship in You.

Life is partly what we make it,
and partly it is made by the friends we choose.

TRACI MULLINS

PLIABLE AS CLAY

"Can I not do with you, Israel, as this potter does?" declares the Lord.
"Like clay in the hand of the potter, so are you in my hand."

JEREMIAH 18:6 NIV

God, the expert craftsman, has great plans for your life. He created the clay—that is, you. He has a design in mind.

But He won't shape you by force. You must surrender your clay to the Master. Ask yourself what it means to be "like clay in the hand of the potter." Give up selfish claims on fashioning your own design. The clay cannot tell the potter what it intends to be.

Begin by discovering your talents, interests, and strengths. What are the activities you especially enjoy? What skills come naturally to you? Once you discover your unique qualities, turn to observation. Where in your world do you see needs? How are you especially gifted to meet those needs?

Open yourself to being molded into the best version of yourself. God wants to fashion your character, your heart, your life. Let Him.

ANNA GINDLESPERGER

Lord, forgive me for selfishly holding back my talents and gifts.
Reveal my strengths, and may I use them to better serve You.

Our gifts and talents are the things people
celebrate about us, but we find to be no big deal,
because the ability comes naturally to us.
That is why it is called a gift.

MICHELLE McKINNEY HAMMOND

MOOSE

God made the wild animals according to their kinds.

GENESIS 1:25 NIV

I know God has a sense of humor. He did, after all, create the moose, which looks like a horse gone incredibly wrong.

I met my first moose in the middle of an isolated logging road. We rounded a blind bend a little too fast, coming face-to-knee with a young animal who stood his ground in true moose fashion. My first thought was, *He's so big!* Television or photographs do not convey the sheer massiveness of a moose, even a young one.

Moose are not overly intelligent. Fortunately, they are exceedingly calm, collected animals, curious and patient with humans who invade their space. This particular moose blocked the road for a good ten minutes to look us over before ambling off into the bushes.

No human who has ever shared space with a moose can avoid loving them. They are somewhat like an ugly baby—always a surprise, but one that makes you smile. God didn't make the moose beautiful or smart, just irresistible, and seeing a moose can only be considered a blessing.

TONI SORTOR

Thank You, God,
for the unexpected delight of a moose.

Taking delight in random encounters
that come our way is a wonderful reminder
that God is in control.

MEL LAWRENZ

Keep Your Vision

Where there is no vision, the people perish.

Proverbs 29:18 KJV

I've seen it happen with people who retire early in life. They lose their drive, their vision, their reason for getting up in the morning. But you don't have to be of retirement age to lose your vision. The devil loves to discourage all of us and steal our hope.

No matter where we are in life, we need to have a goal, a dream, a vision. If we don't, the Word says we'll perish. I don't think it means we'll perish physically, but we'll die spiritually. That's why it's so important to find out God's plan. Do you know God's plan for your life?

If not, ask God to show you His vision for your life. Seek His plan, and once you discover it, write it down, and keep it before you. Thank Him for that vision every day. Keep the vision close to your heart. Your vision is something to be treasured and celebrated.

MICHELLE MEDLOCK ADAMS

Lord, help me to never lose my vision or my drive.
I want to move forward with You.

When we are born again we all have visions,
if we are spiritual at all, of what Jesus wants us to be,
and the great thing is to learn not to be disobedient
to the vision, not to say that it cannot be attained.

OSWALD CHAMBERS

SAVE ME

God, God, save me! I'm in over my head.

PSALM 69:1 MSG

The bills have piled up almost as high as the laundry. You got a traffic ticket. It's pouring. You stand drenched to the bone and begin to shiver in the cold. Tears start to flow down your cheeks, but no one notices. The tears just mingle with the rain, and maybe everyone else is crying also. We are all too busy, too stressed, too frazzled.

"God, God, save me! I'm in over my head," the psalmist wrote. In the twenty-first century, we can relate to his plea!

Come, Father, and lift from me these burdens I've created for myself. Help me to shed some extra burdens in order that I might focus again on what's important, which is You, my God. Help me to rest in Your goodness and Your deep love for me.

EMILY BIGGERS

I am in over my head! I cry out to You. I need You this day,
this hour, this moment. I need the One who made me and knit me
together in my mother's womb to find me here.
I need You to save me, Lord—if even from myself.

Come and yoke yourself with Jesus Christ.
Come and find rest from the burden of your sin.
Come and trade your busy life for His,
because only by the power of the Son of God
will there be rest for your soul.

ANGELA THOMAS McGUFFEY

What a Rush!

Likewise, I say unto you, there is joy in the presence of the angels of God over one sinner that repenteth.

Luke 15:10 kjv

There's no feeling quite like an adrenaline rush. Experiences like riding a roller coaster, bungee jumping, graduation, or getting a new job can result in the heart-pounding excitement adrenaline brings. It's intoxicating! And it always, always makes you want more.

Luke 15 tells us the angels experience that sort of rush when even one sinner repents and turns to God. Do we all feel that way? Are we driven to feel that same rush by witnessing to unbelievers and seeing sinners repent as they turn to God as their Savior?

Challenge yourself to reach out and experience what the angels do when your lifestyle, words, and efforts cause an unbeliever to turn to God. There is no adrenaline rush that even comes close to that one!

Nicole O'Dell

Father, please give me boldness to reach out to others and lead them to You. Give me the words to say, and make the hearer receptive to whatever You lead me to say or do.

Are you winning souls for Jesus?
Does your life example prove
Him to be the precious Savior
Sacrificed because of love?

CARRIE BRECK

An Unexpected Turn

"He makes my way perfect."

2 Samuel 22:33 nkjv

We always want to be in the right place at the right time. Life moves in a hurry, and we thrust ourselves forward into each appointment or commitment. We get frustrated when we miss a turn or mistakenly veer down a wrong road.

What if you put a different spin on the frustration of going out of your way? You can get bent out of shape and become frustrated, or believe that God makes your way perfect and He has kept you from harm's way. What if that wrong turn that you thought cost you ten extra minutes in traffic actually kept you from a fender bender or something worse?

Instead of feeling lost and undone, consider that perhaps this was the path you were destined to take. A series of unfortunate events or a trip down an unexpected path can lead to a positive spin on your day. Be open to taking a different route today. It could open new doors of opportunity.

Shanna D. Gregor

Father, help me to relax,
trusting that You order my steps
and make my way perfect every day.

The Christian walk is a journey.
As we continue on our path,
we come to know a deepening of our faith.
We can eventually see God in
everything and take great comfort in knowing
He is there, even when we don't
understand all that is happening.

BETTIE YOUNGS AND DEBBIE THURMAN

A Personal Counselor

"But the Advocate, the Holy Spirit, whom the Father will send in my name, will teach you all things and will remind you of everything I have said to you."

JOHN 14:26 NIV

Isn't it amazing how the Spirit will sometimes guide you right to a Bible verse, a sermon, a song, or a book containing the very message you need to hear? In a bookstore, you aimlessly meander, flip through books, and unintentionally find one—complete with scriptures to chew on—that addresses issues you've been quietly wrestling with.

While it's not always so blatant, the Spirit moves and flows in our hearts when we open ourselves to Him. Truths that we have stored in our minds are retrieved later by the Spirit, maybe for encouraging a friend or for pulling us through tough times. He connects scriptural principles with life situations to keep us from harm's way, to guide our paths, and to comfort our hearts.

P. J. LEHMAN

Holy Spirit, thank You for being my counselor.
Bring truths to my mind, put words in my mouth,
and guide my paths that I might honor You in all walks of life.

You may have no family, no food, no clothes,
no future, no spouse, no health, or no children,
yet be rich beyond your wildest dreams because
you have the Holy Spirit in your life.

JILL BRISCOE

TIMELESS WISDOM

His wife's name was Abigail. And the woman
was intelligent and beautiful in appearance.

1 SAMUEL 25:3 NASB

Abigail is the only woman in the Bible whose brains are
mentioned before her beauty. And how well she used
them! She stood before a furious king and his army,
calming him with just her words. She returned home
at the end of the day but wisely chose just the right time
to tell her quarrelsome husband the news. Her wisdom
and grace made her so memorable that when her
husband died, David made her his bride.

We can easily believe that women in the Bible have
little to teach us. After all, they lived thousands of years
ago. Yet our concerns are not that different, and the
wisdom to handle those concerns still comes from
the same source. Just as God granted Abigail the
wisdom to soothe a king, He will grant us the
wisdom and intelligence to handle whatever
today's world throws at us.

All we have to do is ask.

RAMONA RICHARDS

Lord, thank You for the blessings in my life.
Grant me wisdom and grace to deal with my life in ways
that reflect my faith in You.

Christ is the true light of the world;
it is through him alone that true wisdom
is imparted to the mind.

JONATHAN EDWARDS

No Matter What

Be thankful in all circumstances, for this is God's will for you who belong to Christ Jesus.

1 Thessalonians 5:18 nlt

Sometimes being thankful seems almost impossible. How can I be thankful when I'm working as hard as I can and I'm still unable to pay off all my debt? How can I be thankful when my car dies, my water pump breaks, or my wallet is stolen?

We often experience hardships that make being thankful difficult.

When Paul wrote this verse, he knew what it was to experience hardships and suffering. But Paul also knew the wonderful power and blessing that come from having a relationship with Christ.

Jesus enables us to be thankful, and Jesus is the cause of our thankfulness. *No matter what happens*, we know that Jesus has given up His life to save ours. He sacrificed Himself on the cross so that we may live life to the fullest. We must *always* be thankful for the love that we experience in Christ Jesus.

Mandy Nydegger

Dear Lord, thank You for Your love.
Please let me be thankful, even in the midst of hardships.
You have blessed me beyond measure.

The first great characteristic of the true Christian
is always a sense of thankfulness
and gratitude to God.

D. MARTYN LLOYD-JONES

EVERYDAY MIRACLES

The LORD said unto him, What is that in thine hand?
And he said, A rod. And he said, Cast it on the ground.
And he cast it on the ground, and it became a serpent.

EXODUS 4:2–3 KJV

For forty years Moses cared for his father-in-law's sheep and carried a rod. He knew everything there was to know about rods. But that was before Moses encountered God in the burning bush.

God commanded Moses to return to Egypt, where he had killed a man, and tell Pharaoh to free thousands of Hebrew slaves. Moses suggested many excellent reasons why he should not do this. But God turned his walking stick into a snake to jar Moses out of his comfort zone.

Like Moses, we serve God with gifts and tools He has given us. We may think we know everything there is to know about them. But God may use the car, the pie recipe, the backyard, or the computer for His kingdom in ways we never imagined.

RACHAEL PHILLIPS

Lord God, we often forget that You have bigger,
better ideas for our lives than any we might conceive.
Help us reach for adventure!

Always remember that,
every time you step out of your comfort zone,
you step into God's comfort zone.

MARK CAHILL

HUMILITY BRINGS GLORY

*"For all those who exalt themselves will be humbled,
and those who humble themselves will be exalted."*

LUKE 14:11 NIV

The tree was bare. Every leaf had been shed. Winter
had arrived. Yet beyond the barren tree, the sun
peeked above the treetops. Dawn was breaking. As the
sun ascended higher, its rays were visible through the
bare branches. Before long, the entire tree was glowing
as the sun's radiance shone through it.

Our lives may seem barren. We may find ourselves
standing alone. But God's glory bursts forth. At just
the right time, He makes His appearance. And His
light shines through because our branches are bare.
Our humility allows others to see the Lord clearly
because the focus is no longer on us but on Him.
When we decrease, the Lord will increase.

Do not view humility with disdain. His glory can only
be revealed when we are humble. Humble yourself before
the Lord, and He will lift you up. He will shine through
you, and you will reflect and make known His glory.

JULIE RAYBURN

*Dear Lord, may humility characterize my life
so that You may be glorified.*

One can so easily become too great to be used by God.
One can never be too small for His service.

CORRIE TEN BOOM

RIGHT PEOPLE—
RIGHT PLACE—RIGHT TIME

And so find favor and high esteem in the sight of God and man.

PROVERBS 3:4 NKJV

When God laid out the blueprint for building your life, He scheduled the right people in the right places at precisely the right times. He provided favor, lined up doors of opportunity, and arranged for perfect connections to help you construct a great life. God's blessings have already been ordered and are placed precisely throughout your life journey.

Now it's up to you to recognize the opportunities and meet each appointment God has for you. Walk by faith, listening to His direction so you can be quick to experience every good and perfect gift. God wants you to experience every favor and rich blessing He's prepared.

By faith, expect blessing to meet you at every turn. Imagine what your future holds when you become determined to step out to greet it according to God's design. Expect the goodness He has planned for you—doors of opportunities are opening for you today!

SHANNA D. GREGOR

Lord, thank You for setting favor and blessing in my path,
and help me to expect it wherever I go and in whatever I do.

Life is not a series of accidents
but a succession of divine appointments.

MARY SOUTHERLAND

LOOK UP

In the morning will I direct my prayer unto thee, and will look up.

PSALM 5:3 KJV

"If you look at the ground, you'll be on the ground," the riding trainer says. Over and over the young girl hears this as she canters her horse and learns to jump fences of graduated heights.

"Steer with your eyes" is another expression she hears. As the horse and rider leap over one hurdle, her eyes are on the next fence ahead. This fixed gaze keeps the twosome moving together and springing over the fences.

The psalmist knows something about the importance of fixing one's gaze. "I will look up," he says. In the morning, he directs his prayer to God and watches and waits.

By going to God in prayer early in the day, we set our perspective for the entire day. Once we have given Him our problems and cares and listened for His voice to speak in our hearts, we have set our eyes on Him as the place we are going.

LEAH SLAWSON

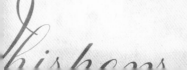

Father, cause me to seek You early each day,
to remember to fix my gaze on You,
and to watch You work in my life.

If we discipline ourselves to have "eyes that see
and ears that hear" and to look up with expectant eyes,
we will find God at work in many different
ways throughout our lives.

BETTY SOUTHARD

CARE ENOUGH TO CONFRONT

Better is open rebuke than hidden love.

PROVERBS 27:5 NIV

Friendships don't always go smoothly. Some days we're in close accord, but other days, little seems to go right, and misunderstanding easily comes between us.

But even those times of disagreement may benefit friends. Perhaps when friendships aren't so touchy-feely, we can be more honest with each other. The hidden irritants that sometimes crop up in relationships can be confronted and dealt with.

Whatever rebuke we receive, isn't it better from a friend who cares for our feelings than from a stranger or enemy? Even if that friendship remains tense for a while, caring can return. What if that friend neglected to tell us an unpleasant truth we really needed to hear?

Let's listen to the courageous love of friends and avoid those who only want to please. The rebuke we face could change our lives for good.

PAMELA L. MCQUADE

Lord, I don't need a bunch of yes-women as my friends.
Give me relationships with those who care enough to confront me.
I need Your truth in all my friendships.

Being confronted on character issues isn't pleasant.
It hurts our self-image. It humbles us.
But it doesn't harm us. Loving confrontation
protects us from blindness and
self-destructiveness.

HENRY CLOUD AND JOHN TOWNSEND

WHAT'S IN YOUR HEART?

*Delight thyself also in the Lord; and he shall give thee
the desires of thine heart.*

PSALM 37:4 KJV

What is it that you most desire? A successful career
or large bank account? Someone with whom you can
share romantic dinners or scenic bike rides? It really
doesn't matter. What does matter is that you are fully
committed to God. When that is the case, the desires
in your heart will be the ones He places there. He will
grant them because they honor Him.

Too many times we look at God's promises as
some sort of magic formula. We fail to realize that His
promises have more to do with our own relationship
with Him. The promise in Psalm 37:4 isn't intended
for personal gain. It is meant to glorify God.

God wants to give you the desires of your heart
when they line up with His perfect plan. As you delight
in Him, His desires will become your desires, and you
will be greatly blessed.

RACHEL QUILLIN

Lord, I know You want to give me the desires of my heart.
Help me live in a way that makes this possible.

What I delight in determines what I desire.
If I delight in God, my desire will be
to do things according to His will
and to ask according to His will.

JOHN MAXWELL

FINDING YOUR FIRST LOVE

Nevertheless I have somewhat against thee,
because thou hast left thy first love.

REVELATION 2:4 KJV

If any church was zealous for Christ, it was the church at Ephesus. Here was a church planted by the apostle Paul and pastored by Timothy. It did not faint from the work of the Gospel. The people of Ephesus *labored* for the Lord. But they became consumed by their labor and forgot that they were ultimately working for the Lord.

We are in danger of falling into the same trap today. As we pour ourselves into living a godly life, we can easily get consumed with the task. Soon we can forget the very One we want to model.

Why God would want to fellowship with us is a great mystery, but He does. He has gone to great lengths to do so. He sent His Son to the cross to make it possible. How can we neglect so great a love?

Today, put aside life's never-ending demands. Open your Bible and return to your first love.

HELEN W. MIDDLEBROOKE

*"Out of myself to dwell in thy love, out of despair
into raptures above. . . Jesus, I come to thee."*

Get up every day, love God,
and do your best.

JOYCE MEYER

GOOD FOR THE SOUL

When I kept silent about my sin, my body wasted away
through my groaning all day long.

PSALM 32:3 NASB

The shame was too great to bear. Tina could hardly
lift her head, let alone face her family. For weeks she
was miserable. Finally, she gathered the courage to talk
with her mother. Tina was shocked when her mother
received her with open arms. A weight had been lifted
from her shoulders. She was forgiven.

Shame is a powerful silencer. When we feel guilty
about our actions, the last thing we want to do is speak
of them. However, Psalm 32:3 reminds us of the pain
silence can cause.

God does not want His children to live in silent
shame. Saying what we've done wrong out loud is
the first step to healing. While other people may not
always forgive us, God promises that if we confess
our sins He will forgive us and cleanse us from our
unrighteousness.

Grace. A clean slate. It's ours for the asking.

JOANNA BLOSS

Father, thank You for the gift of grace,
the promise of forgiveness, and the healing You provide.

At times of greatest shame, we need to do
the exact opposite of what we feel like doing.
We need to lift our faces to our God, open our mouths
in confession, let Him wash us with
forgiveness and bathe us with His radiance.

BETH MOORE

MOUTH FILTER

Nor should there be obscenity, foolish talk or coarse joking,
which are out of place, but rather thanksgiving.

EPHESIANS 5:4 NIV

Does your mouth filter ever quit working? You know, the filter that keeps you from saying the things you're thinking? Mine goes out from time to time. That's when I suffer from "foot in mouth" disease. That happened to me not long ago when I asked a lady when her baby was due and she informed me that she wasn't pregnant. Ouch! Okay, from now on, unless a woman is wearing a "Baby on Board" T-shirt, I'm never asking that question again!

Sometimes, we say things without thinking. We don't mean to say them; they just come out before we can retrieve them. Many times, those words can be hurtful. So, think before you speak. Run it through your Holy Spirit filter before uttering a single syllable. Ask the Lord to help you say only uplifting, encouraging, and wise words.

MICHELLE MEDLOCK ADAMS

*Heavenly Father,
help me to develop my Holy Spirit filter.*

To guard the passion and presence of God
in your heart, choose your words the
way you choose your friends. . .wisely.
Know they will be few but precious.

LISA BEVERE

THE PERFECT REFLECTION

"Give careful thought to your ways."

HAGGAI 1:7 NIV

You probably know how it feels to have a bad hair day or a huge zit on your face. On days like these, we try to avoid the mirror.

Our Christian lives often have a similar feel. Instead of facing our imperfections, we work hard to avoid any mention of or allusion to them. God's command to give careful thought to our ways may fill us with dread because the reflection can be so unattractive.

We should first look back and reflect on God's work in our lives. We are on a journey. We must consider where we were when God found us and where we are now through His grace. We must think about the ways our present actions, habits, and attitude toward God reflect our lives as Christians.

Only when we are able to honestly assess our lives in Christ, can we call on His name to help perfect our reflection.

MANDY NYDEGGER

*Dear Lord, help me to look honestly at the ways
I live and make changes where necessary.*

To acknowledge your imperfections
does not mean you are a failure;
it is an admission that you are human.

GARY CHAPMAN

SMILE, SMILE, SMILE

"I will forget my complaint,
I will change my expression, and smile."

JOB 9:27 NIV

Jenni had been having a bad day. Everything seemed to go wrong from the moment she awoke. Then something happened. A man on the sidewalk smiled at her and opened the door to her office. It wasn't much, but that small gesture helped lighten her mood.

Days may not go just as planned. We are all human, and we can't always control our circumstances. What we can control, however, is our attitude. Remember each day that you are a representative of Jesus Christ. As a Christian and a woman, it is important to model a godly attitude at all times. Even a small look or smile can help show others the love of God.

Just because we don't feel like having a good attitude, doesn't mean we shouldn't try. God tells us to praise Him always—in good times and in bad. Let that praise show on your face today.

CHRISTAN M. THOMAS

Lord, I know I can choose my attitude. Help me to show Your love
to others by having a positive attitude each day.
Let Your glory show on my face.

We make the decision as to whether the events
of our life will serve as stepping stones
or stumbling blocks.

MAXIE DUNHAM

MORE BLESSED TO GIVE

"Give, and it will be given to you. A good measure, pressed down,
shaken together and running over, will be poured into your lap.
For with the measure you use, it will be measured to you."

LUKE 6:38 NIV

When Cassie learned that her church's homeless ministry needed help, she volunteered, anxious to give what she could.

Lending a hand seemed like the right thing to do, and she expected to find lots of needy people with whom she could share her gifts. She found plenty of needy people. However, what she hadn't expected was to be blessed so much. Not only did she make some new friends, but they taught her a great deal about thankfulness.

In God's economy, giving means receiving. When we give, we receive more than the satisfaction of a job well done. Jesus promises blessing when we give. Getting something shouldn't be our motivation for serving others, but it is an added bonus. What can *you* do today to be a blessing to others?

JOANNA BLOSS

Lord, thank You for the promise of giving and receiving.
Help me to bless others as You have blessed me.

We never outgrow our need for others.
In fact, giving ourselves to help others is even more
life building than receiving help from others.
The law of living is giving.

GEORGE SWEETING

FINDING REAL REST

And I said, Oh that I had wings like a dove!
for then would I fly away, and be at rest.

PSALM 55:6 KJV

There are days. . .
- when the phone doesn't stop ringing.
- when your favorite sweater ends up in the dryer.
- when you think things can't get any worse, but they do.

On such days, it's tempting to wish for an easy way out. If only you could fly away! Then you could be at rest. Really?

It takes more than a quiet place or a time away to bring true rest. Often, even if we go away from the noise and demands, instead of being at peace, we're full of guilt and regret. Instead of flying away, we must jump into God's everlasting arms and dive into His Word. Rest is found in knowing Christ and understanding that through His sacrifice, we are at peace.

HELEN W. MIDDLEBROOKE

Father God, there are many days when I don't have time to sit. In all these times, remind me that peace comes from knowing You and resting in the work You have done.

The Bible commands us to rest. . . .
What a generous and kind God we have.
We expect marching orders, or hoops
to jump through. But God simply says,
"Alright, this will be challenging, but here's
what I want you to do: take a break."

KERI WYATT KENT

SECOND THOUGHTS

"He is like the light of morning at sunrise on a cloudless morning."

2 SAMUEL 23:4 NIV

Mid-January, just about dawn, the sun barely began to lift its head over the hills to the east. I could tell that much before I pulled back the drapes.

What I saw next took my breath away. We had had an ice storm overnight, and the world was ablaze with diamonds. Horizontal rays of sun threw every tree branch into sharp detail. Icicles glittered below every mundane surface. My first thought was, *Wow! Thank You, Lord!*

My second thought was, *Wonder if I'll be stuck in the house all day. I have to get to the store.* The glorious sight had not changed, but my perception had, and some of the overwhelming magic had lost its sheen.

Second thoughts do that to us. Our rational minds slide right past moments of glory and anchor us to firm reality. That's not all bad, but we need to train ourselves not to let blessings slip away before we enjoy them and thank the Lord for giving us a glimpse of His glory.

TONI SORTOR

Lord, keep Your "Wow" in my day.

I'm often reminded of God's glory when I see fireworks exploding in the night sky, illuminating everything around with breathtaking beauty and power.

PRESTON PARRISH

GET A LIFE

In him was life, and that life was the light of all mankind.

JOHN 1:4 NIV

Do you have a life?

You've probably been asked that more than once. Having a life usually means you have a busy social calendar. The world tells us that brings happiness and fulfillment.

The Bible defines having a life a bit differently. In John 14:6, Jesus tells us that He is the way, the truth, and the life. He is our only way to our Father in heaven and the only One who can fill us with real life.

So, do you have the light of Christ living inside you, or do you need to get a life? A place to go, things to do, and people to see don't mean a whole lot at the end of your life here on earth. You will never look back and wish you attended one more social event. Jesus is the only way to eternal life. Make sure you've got a life before you leave!

MARILEE PARRISH

Dear Jesus, I want You to light up
my soul and give me eternal life.
Help me to live my life for You.

We are all the time coming to the end of things
here—the end of the week, the end of the month,
the end of the year, the end of school days.
It is end, end, end all the time. But, thank God,
He is going to satisfy us with long life;
no end to it, an endless life.

D. L. MOODY

It's about Time

There's an opportune time to do things, a right time for everything on the earth.

ECCLESIASTES 3:1 MSG

Our schedules keep us moving from early in the morning until late at night. Every task—and often free time—needs to be penciled into our calendar.

What makes the top of your list of priorities? Spending time with friends? Going to the gym? What about reading the Bible? Attending church?

While there is nothing wrong with doing any of these things, we need to assess whether we have our priorities in order. We only have twenty-four hours in each day.

Of course, God needs to be given first place. That doesn't necessarily mean that devotions should be done first thing in the morning, but it means devotional time should be set apart. After determining that, list your activities and prioritize them.

You may find you need to eliminate some things from your schedule in order to slow down the pace of life a bit. Pray about it—God will help you with the choices you need to make.

JENNIFER HAHN

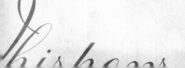

Dear Father, please be the Lord of my schedule.
Give me wisdom in determining my priorities.

A successful life is lived by one who has the
right priorities in his life—being obedient to
God's Word—and then putting into action
what he knows to be true.

BOB AND EMILIE BARNES

HE IS FAITHFUL

If we are unfaithful, he remains faithful,
for he cannot deny who he is.

2 TIMOTHY 2:13 NLT

Have you ever said you'll do something, knowing full well you probably wouldn't get it done? We humans have a knack for letting each other down.

Sometimes we treat our relationship with God the same as we do with other people. We promise Him we'll start spending more time with Him in prayer and Bible study. *This time, it will be different—I'll stick with it*, we think. Soon the daily distractions of life get in the way, and we're back in our same routine, minus prayer and Bible study.

Even when we fail to live up to our expectations, our heavenly Father doesn't pick up His judge's gavel and condemn us for unfaithfulness. He remains a faithful supporter, encouraging us to hold up our end of the bargain. Take comfort in His faithfulness, and let that encourage you toward a deeper relationship with Him.

ANNIE TIPTON

Father, thank You for Your unending faithfulness.
Every day I fall short of Your standards,
but You're always there,
encouraging me and lifting me up.

You and I can go to God when we are too tired,
too lazy, too uncommitted, too sick,
or feeling too sorry for ourselves.
In fact, moments like these are precisely
when we need to call upon God
and be filled with His faithfulness.

ELIZABETH GEORGE

LEAVE YOUR BAGS BEHIND

Give all your worries and cares to God, for he cares about you.

1 PETER 5:7 NLT

Imagine your best friend announced she's treating you to an all-expenses-paid cruise. All your meals are included, and she's throwing in a brand-new wardrobe.

"Leave your bags behind," she tells you. "All you have to do is show up."

Can you imagine arriving at the cruise ship with full suitcases? "Why are you carrying all this junk?" your friend would say. "I told you I had it covered—don't you trust me?"

All too often, this is how we approach God. He invites us to give Him our burdens, but we show up weighed down with bags. Worry, anger, resentment, and anxious thoughts slow us down so that we're not productive.

God told us to give all our cares to Him. He promises He has them covered, yet we still hang on.

What baggage are you carrying today that you can give to the Lord?

JOANNA BLOSS

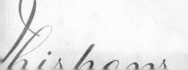

Father, thank You for the invitation to cast all my cares upon You.
Help me to let go of the things that weigh me down
and trust You to take them for me.

God's rescue plan—to be delivered,
you have to let go.

SHEILA WALSH

THANKFUL SPEECH

Give thanks to the Lord, for he is good; his love endures forever.

PSALM 107:1 NIV

Have you ever heard the expression, "You better thank your lucky stars!" You may have even said it a time or two. Or how about, "Well, thank goodness!" Funny how sayings slip into our speech without our really giving them much thought. But we really should be careful with our speech—especially when we're dishing out thanks.

When something good happens, don't thank your lucky stars or goodness—they didn't have anything to do with it! Thank your loving heavenly Father who lavishly blesses you every day. Get into the habit of immediately recognizing the Lord for His goodness right when it happens. If I get a parking spot up front at Walmart, I say, "Thank You, Lord, for holding that spot just for me."

Make thanking God a habit, and you'll find that you have many reasons to praise Him. It puts you in an attitude of gratitude, and that's a great place to be!

MICHELLE MEDLOCK ADAMS

Thank You, Lord, for everything You do for me each day.
Help me to be better at recognizing every blessing that You send my way.

We can thank God for everything good,
and all the rest we don't comprehend yet.

KRISTIN ARMSTRONG

GENUINE ARTICLE

*"Whoever speaks on their own does so to gain personal glory,
but he who seeks the glory of the one who sent him is a man of truth;
there is nothing false about him."*

JOHN 7:18 NIV

Amy isn't swayed by the opinion of others. She doesn't have to always be the center of attention. Knowing the job is done for God's glory is enough.

Is she stiff or boring? On the contrary—she's refreshing! There is nothing fake about her. She has the freedom to be who God created her to be. She is liked and respected as Christ shines through her.

Self-promoters push their way through. They can be shallow and a pain to be around. Christ-promoters are secure in not having to receive accolades. Their freedom and authenticity outshine the self-absorbed heart.

By focusing on Christ and the glory He deserves, we allow God to produce in us an enriched life as a person of truth.

P. J. LEHMAN

God, sometimes I find I am promoting myself rather than giving You the honor. Help me to be all I am created to be because You are foremost in my heart.

Let us watch against unbelief, pride,
and self-confidence. If we go forth in our own strength,
we shall faint, and utterly fall; but having our hearts
and our hopes in heaven, we shall be carried above all
difficulties, and be enabled to lay hold of the prize
of our high calling in Christ Jesus.

MATTHEW HENRY

ALWAYS THINKING OF YOU

What is man that You are mindful of him,
and the son of man that You visit him?

PSALM 8:4 NKJV

What are you thinking about today? Do you have a
list of things you want to get done, people you need
to call, or maybe a vacation you want to plan? Your
thoughts fill up your days and keep you busy.

Have you ever wondered what God thinks about?
He thinks about you! You are always on His mind.
In all you think and do, He considers you and makes
intercession for you. He knows the thoughts and intents
of your heart. He's constantly aware of your feelings and
how you interact with or without Him each day.

God is always with you, waiting for you to
remember Him—to call on Him for help, for
friendship, for anything you need. He wants to be
a big part of your life. And if you include Him,
He will open the doors to as much goodness,
mercy, and love as you'll allow Him to
bless you with.

SHANNA D. GREGOR

*Lord, help me to include You in my life
and always be thinking of You, too.*

The mind in love with God is engaged
with God's thoughts and ways, just as a lover
is engaged with the words and actions
of the beloved.

NANCY NORDENSON

CONSOLATION AMID CONFLICT

Our bodies had no rest, but we were troubled on every side.
Outside were conflicts, inside were fears. Nevertheless God,
who comforts the downcast, comforted us by the coming of Titus.

2 CORINTHIANS 7:5–6 NKJV

Sometimes we feel so beaten down by life, battered by uncontrollable outside circumstances. Fear permeates our inner beings. Seeing no way out, we may fall into depression, withdrawing into ourselves. We cut ourselves off from those who would give us aid and comfort.

Fortunately, God has other plans. He knows what we need and lovingly provides it. He sends earthly angels to help us. These people of God give freely of God's love and fill us with the healing balm of His comfort.

In the midst of distress, we are not to withdraw from God's helping hand but immerse ourselves in His Word and reach out to others, allowing both to give us love and comfort in our time of need. And then, whole once more, we in turn can be a Titus for another.

DONNA K. MALTESE

*Dear God, You know my frame, my circumstances,
my outlook, my troubles. Comfort me in this situation
through Your Word and the love of others.*

God doesn't comfort us to make us comfortable,
but to make us comforters.

BILLY GRAHAM

BREATHING ROOM

He's solid rock under my feet, breathing room for my soul,
an impregnable castle.

PSALM 62:2 MSG

In a materialistic, ambitious society like ours, the idea of taking time to rest and play isn't always our highest priority. After all, we're told that to get ahead you have to work longer and harder than everyone else.

But God formed us with a need for downtime. So don't let a fear of falling behind rob you of the joy and necessity of recreation. Our bodies and souls need fun in order to thrive.

Find some way to blow off steam. What did you like to do as a child? Answering that question can guide you to a hobby that relaxes you and gives you deep, abiding joy.

And as believers, we can—and should—invite God into our recreation times. He wants to be a part of every area of our daily lives. After all, He is the place where our souls find their ultimate rest and peace.

DENA DYER

Father, I praise You for the way You made me—
with a need to work, rest, and play.
I invite You to join me while I recreate.

Thou hast made us for Thyself, O Lord,
and our hearts are restless until
they rest in Thee.

SAINT AUGUSTINE

GOD'S WASH DAY

*If we confess our sins, he is faithful and just to forgive us our sins,
and to cleanse us from all unrighteousness.*

1 JOHN 1:9 KJV

Women know all about wash day: the piles of sorted clothes; the cleaning products; the time it takes to wash, dry, and fold. Most of us work it in around other chores to make the most of our time, but it still doesn't happen quickly. Even when we do our best, sometimes a few items don't come out quite clean and need rewashing.

Did you realize that God does laundry, too? But He needs nothing out of a box or bottle. His cleansing works not on fabric but on human hearts. The "detergent" is the blood of His Son.

Ironically, blood causes a stain that is hard to remove from clothes. But the blood of Jesus eradicates all the dirt on human hearts. No matter how often we fail, we can return, and a simple confession will renew the cleansing.

Need a wash? Look to God.

PAMELA L. MCQUADE

*Thank You, Lord, for washing my heart
clean with Your own blood.*

To confess your sins to God is not to tell God anything
God doesn't already know. Until you confess them,
however, they are the abyss between you.
When you confess them,
they become the Golden Gate Bridge.

FREDERICK BUECHNER

FRIENDSHIP

*"I have called you friends, for everything that
I learned from my Father I have made known to you."*

JOHN 15:15 NIV

No one seems to have time for friendship these days.
Everyone is overscheduled, and you have to invest time
to allow a friendship to blossom. Finding a friend is as
challenging as finding a spouse.

There are also various levels of friendship to
consider. Casual friendships are easy. But these
superficial friendships soon die if they move away or
children transfer to a different school. They're like a
nice dessert, but they aren't very enriching.

Then there are serious friendships that can endure
anything, forgive everything. Once acquired, friends like
these are precious blessings. In times of tragedy, they will
listen to you cry and cry with you. In good times,
you will want to share your joy with them, and your
happiness will make them happy. Good friends
are nourishment for the heart and soul.
Take the time to build such friendships,
and you will never be lonely again.

TONI SORTOR

Lord, build my friendships with me.

Friendship is like love.
It cannot be demanded or driven or insisted upon.
It must be wooed to be won.

LAURA INGALLS WILDER

BUSY WAITING

*"Not one of these men, this evil generation,
shall see the good land which I swore to give your fathers."*

DEUTERONOMY 1:35 NASB

For forty years, those woeful Israelites wandered
through the desert to reach the Promised Land. How
often they must have stared down at a valley or looked
to the mountain summits, dreading the thousands
of steps required to get to there. Scholars have
determined that forty-year journey should have taken
only three days—at the very most, two weeks.

That generation of Israelites had no real purpose
to their lives. They were busy people, but faithless. No
Bible verses applaud their lives. It's as if they never
lived at all. Despite witnessing miracle after miracle,
they never saw those tests as opportunities to trust God
in a deeper way. What wasted lives!

And what a lesson to the rest of us! Are we trusting and
depending on God in deeper ways throughout our full
and busy days? Or are we merely moving from one spot to
the next, productive, but not purposeful—busy waiting?

SUZANNE WOODS FISHER

Lord, I want my life to count!
With single-hearted devotion, may I look to You in all things.

Those who have stations of importance to fill,
have generally so many indispensable duties to perform,
that without the greatest care in the management of
their time, none will be left to be alone with God.

FRANÇOIS FÉNELON AND JEANNE GUYON

HERE COMES THE JUDGE

I can do all this through him who gives me strength.

PHILIPPIANS 4:13 NIV

Do you worry about what others think of you? Most women struggle with feeling judged—even gorgeous, "got it all together" women. One of my absolutely beautiful friends once said, "I'd love to do more teaching, but I'm just not ready."

I started thinking, *If she's not ready, nobody is ready.* I said, "You are *so* ready.

She sighed.

"What's the problem?"

"I have to lose fifteen more pounds before I'll be ready. Everyone will be looking at how big my behind is rather than focusing on the message."

I couldn't believe my ears. The devil had so deceived her.

Have insecurities and fear kept you from doing great things for God? If so, just give those concerns to God, and ask Him to fill you with His love and confidence.

MICHELLE MEDLOCK ADAMS

Lord, keep me from worrying about how others judge me.
You are my only judge.

Our call is to a holy confidence and
humble dependence: we are to walk through
life with our heads high, knowing it is Jesus who
loves us and qualifies us for His purposes.

SUSIE LARSON

GOD HAS CONFIDENCE IN YOU

He delivered me from my strong enemy, and from them which hated me. . . .
They prevented me in the day of my calamity: but the Lord was my stay.
He brought me forth also into a large place; he delivered me,
because he delighted in me.

PSALM 18:17–19 KJV

How many times have your prayers been answered?
How many times has God taken care of you? Your
friends and family? How many times has it "worked
out," when others thought it would not?

At some point in our lives, our obstacles, our
"calamities," may prevent us from following the true
path God has ordained for us. Yet, if we trust in the
Lord and give our lives over to Him, we can clearly
see "He brought me forth also into a large place; he
delivered me, because he delighted in me."

Think about that! He *delights* in us! By believing
in God's grace and love, by trusting Him, we find
confidence to deal with our troubles out of the infinite
hope, strength, and wisdom that comes from loving the
Lord. Nothing pleases God more.

RAMONA RICHARDS

Lord, help me to please You by trusting in Your deliverance.

No storm is so great, no wave is so high,
no sea is so deep, no wind is so strong,
that Jesus cannot either calm it or carry us through it.

ANNE GRAHAM LOTZ

INSIDE OUT

In like manner also, that women adorn themselves in modest apparel,
with shamefacedness and sobriety; not with broided hair, or gold, or pearls,
or costly array; but (which becometh women professing godliness)
with good works.

1 TIMOTHY 2:9–10 KJV

Is it wrong to want to look nice? No! The point of
this verse is not that women should look frumpy
and unattractive. However, being well-dressed is
completely pointless if inner beauty is absent.

It is possible to be neatly, even stylishly, attired
and still be modest. Your makeup and jewelry can be
applied neatly and with good taste but not in a way that
draws unnecessary attention to yourself.

Your purpose is to be godly—to draw people to
Jesus. You do this by walking so closely with Him that
His beauty is reflected in You. Designer clothes
and expensive accessories are worthless—an
artificial beauty—if Christ's love is not
radiating through your entire being.

Get your priorities straight. Be sure
your heart is beautiful, and external
attractiveness is sure to follow.

RACHEL QUILLIN

Lord Jesus, let Your love shine through me.
May my heart be beautiful in Thy sight.

Believers are not to use outward appearance as the
main criterion by which to evaluate the women
of the Bible, or anyone else, for that matter.
Though physical appearance is important to people,
it is not God's standard for evaluation.

PAT WARREN

WELL-SEASONED
SPEECH

*Let your conversation be always full of grace, seasoned with salt,
so that you may know how to answer everyone.*

COLOSSIANS 4:6 NIV

Cassie was a horrible cook! Her food was bland, flat, and boring—no zest, no zing to tempt you for a second helping. She'd try to please people with what they wanted, but the result was pathetic.

As pale and uninviting as Cassie's food was, her conversations were the exact opposite: full of life, spiced with the hope of the Gospel, meaty with truth, and sprinkled with kindness and love. People were drawn to her and would linger, savoring the sweet aroma of Christ that bubbled from within her. She used words that encouraged, challenged, or piqued you for more.

When asked about this, Cassie admitted to making every effort to choose words that build people up or make them laugh—a practice of longer-lasting value than cuisine acclaim.

P. J. LEHMAN

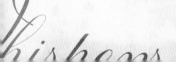

Word Giver, may Your words of truth and life be on my lips.
Help me sprinkle the salt of grace on those I converse with,
making them want more of You.

Genuinely encouraging words are ones that
communicate the idea, *I know who you are;*
I care about you, and I'm here to help you.

GARY CHAPMAN

DONE IN BY DELILAH

She sent and called for the lords of the Philistines, saying,
Come up this once, for he hath shewed me all his heart.
Then the lords of the Philistines came up unto her,
and brought money in their hand.

JUDGES 16:18 KJV

As a girl, Delilah discovered her smile could get her whatever she wanted.

As a beautiful woman, Delilah wanted Samson. Samson's tendency to worship his God annoyed Delilah, but he amused her. For a while, it was enough.

One day Philistine leaders offered her money to learn the secret of Samson's strength. Delilah used every word, look, and movement to torture him into telling her. Finally, Samson told her that if his hair was cut, his strength would disappear. Delilah lulled him to sleep then called for a barber—and the Philistine lords who blinded Samson and chained him to a treadmill like a beast.

What a sad ending to romance. What if Delilah had used her beauty and persuasion to inspire Samson to serve God?

RACHAEL PHILLIPS

Father, You have given me special influence, too.
Help me bless others and point them to You.

If you concern yourself with your
neighbor's talents, you will neglect yours.
But if you concern yourself with yours,
you could inspire both.
MAX LUCADO

DEFEAT DOOM AND GLOOM

"Do not sorrow, for the joy of the Lord is your strength."

NEHEMIAH 8:10 NKJV

Do you know a person who is a "gloom and doomer"? You know the type—the person who *never* has a good day. The person you never ask, "How are you?" because you'll be there listening to her misfortunes, bad luck, and illnesses for hours. Maybe you're a gloom-and-doom kind of gal. If you are, there's hope.

You don't have to live with a dark cloud over your head anymore. God is your way out of gloom and doom. He will help you make joyful living a way of life.

Determine today to become a positive person. Let's get all the gloom and doom out of our lives once and for all. Get in the habit of saying these confessions every day: "I am well able to fulfill my destiny. God has made me an overcomer. No weapon formed against me is going to prosper. The joy of the Lord is my strength." Before long, that dark cloud that's been blocking the Son is sure to move out!

MICHELLE MEDLOCK ADAMS

Lord, help me to be a positive person.

God created you in His own image,
and He wants you to experience
His joy and abundance.
But God will not force His joy upon you;
you must claim it.

BETH MOORE

Help in the Midst of Trouble

*"We do not know what to do,
but we are looking to you for help."*

2 Chronicles 20:12 NLT

King Jehoshaphat's army was in big trouble. Several surrounding nations had declared war on Israel, and a battle was imminent. King Jehoshaphat immediately called on his people to fast and pray. God answered the prayers of Jehoshaphat and his people by causing the enemy armies to attack each other. As the Israelites marched into battle singing praises to God, they found that not one of the enemy had survived.

So often in this world, we come face-to-face with experiences that overwhelm us. Life is full of situations that seem insurmountable. Like Jehoshaphat and the Israelites, God desires that we rely on Him for all our needs. Trust that God will hear your prayers. Depend on Him to listen and answer. Believe that God will not allow you to be overcome by your trials; instead, He will faithfully and lovingly bring you through to the other side.

Mandy Nydegger

Dear Lord, thank You for Your faithfulness.
When I am overwhelmed,
let me look to You for guidance and help.

We all get caught up in the daily details of life,
and it can hinder our seeing the bigger plan
God has for us. Our immediate problems
overwhelm us and seem to obliterate
God's promises. God, on the other hand,
sees the bigger picture and wants us to focus
in on what he is accomplishing in our lives.

BETTY SOUTHARD

A DAY OF REST

Six days thou shalt do thy work, and on the seventh day thou shalt rest:
that thine ox and thine ass may rest, and the son of thy handmaid,
and the stranger, may be refreshed.

EXODUS 23:12 KJV

If there is one scriptural principle women routinely abandon, it is that of the Sabbath. Because Christ has become our rest and we now worship on the Lord's Day, we often disregard the idea of a Sabbath rest. One day out of seven, God's people were not to work or to make others work, so they could all be refreshed.

God Himself started the work-rest pattern before the earth was a week old. God didn't rest because He was tired; He rested because His work of creation was finished.

But a woman's work is never done! How can she rest?

It's not easy. There are always more things that can be done. But most of those things can wait a day while you recharge.

God's design for the week gives rest to the weary. Let's not neglect His provision.

HELEN W. MIDDLEBROOKE

Father, help me to rest from my labor as You rested from Yours.

It's the rests that make the difference in the music of our lives. They really are the pauses that refresh.

Steve and Mary Farrar

ENCOURAGED

Be kind and compassionate to one another.

EPHESIANS 4:32 NIV

Do you know that some people never hear a "thank-you"?

You'll be able to spot these folks. They are usually the grouchy ones. I encountered one the other day at a shoe store. She was checking me out (with a scowl on her face) when I noticed she had charged me full price for my shoes. So I said, "Miss, according to that sign over there, these shoes are on sale for 30 percent off."

"These aren't the same shoes."

"I think they are," I said, "because I checked the SKU number against the advertisement."

She stomped over to the sale area and did her own investigation. After a few minutes, she came back, still scowling, and said, "You're right. They are on sale. I'll have to redo the whole transaction."

It was obvious she was having a hard day. So, I made it my mission to encourage her. I thanked her for redoing my receipt. We ended up having a nice conversation. She even smiled. Make it your mission to appreciate someone today.

MICHELLE MEDLOCK ADAMS

Lord, help me to seize every
opportunity to bless others.

All who have received grace should learn
to be gracious to others.

WATCHMAN NEE

LETTING GO

Clothe yourselves with compassion, kindness, humility, gentleness and patience. Bear with each other and forgive one another if any of you has a grievance against someone. Forgive as the Lord forgave you.

COLOSSIANS 3:12–13 NIV

Christine knew she needed to forgive her friend Sandy. However, she couldn't stop rehearsing the ordeal in her mind. How could Sandy have been so thoughtless? The harder Christine tried to make herself forgive, the further away forgiveness seemed.

Then Sandy's father died, and Christine decided to take her a meal. As Christine prepared the casserole, she found herself praying for Sandy. Feelings of injustice were gradually replaced by kindness and compassion. By the time Christine arrived to deliver the meal, she'd forgiven Sandy.

We speak of working toward forgiveness, but perhaps we would do better to work toward feeling genuine Christlike compassion for others, treating them with kindness and patience, and praying that God would help us to see others through His eyes. One day we will wake up and realize that forgiveness has replaced our pain.

JOANNA BLOSS

God, how grateful I am that You have forgiven me.
Please help me to see, through Your eyes,
the person who has wronged me.

Some of the sweetest words in the world,
no matter what language, are those that say,
"I forgive you."

KAY ARTHUR

TREASURES OF LOVE

He chose us in Him before the foundation of the world,
that we would be holy and blameless before Him.

EPHESIANS 1:4 NASB

God sees us the way we seldom see ourselves—holy, pure, and blameless.

It seems impossible. Did He forget the day we impatiently shifted back and forth in line, sending mental daggers to the person ahead who moved too slowly? Or all the times we complain and fret when our plans do not unfold in the way we hope?

We start our day with good intentions. But in our rush to achieve and be, we miss the mark, not seeing that who we are has already been named. We have already been claimed.

Picked out of the refuse of our failures, we are restored and covered in a blanket of His grace. Set apart for a glorious purpose, we are bestowed with the jewels of His love. It is not He who forgets, but rather we who need to remember. We are His living treasure here on earth.

SARAH HAWKINS

Father, help me to reflect Your love through my words and deeds so that when others see me, they really see You.

It is important for every Christian to keep in mind the great difference between his position and his practice, his standing and his state. God sees us as righteous, because He sees us through His righteous Son, who has taken our place, and because He has planted in us a righteous new nature.

JOHN MACARTHUR

PRAISE FEST

In the morning, Lord, you hear my voice; in the morning I lay my requests before you and wait expectantly.

PSALM 5:3 NIV

How do you start your mornings? Do you roll out of bed, grumbling and grumpy, or spring out of bed, praising the Lord? If you're like me, you're not exactly chipper in the morning. But I'm learning to like those early hours a little better. Why? Because mornings are a great time to praise the Lord!

If you start your day giving praises to God, it's even more energizing than a shot of espresso. No matter how grumpy you feel, once you start praising God for His love and His goodness, you're bound to change your mood for the better.

So, why not use your mouth for something worthwhile? Begin each day thanking God. It will take some practice, but you'll get the hang of it. The Holy Spirit will help you. Praise God for the many blessings in your life. Praise Him just because He is God and deserving of our praise. If you do, the mornings will be a lot brighter.

MICHELLE MEDLOCK ADAMS

Lord, I praise You for who You are.

I must never lose that sense of wonder and awe
when I come into the presence of God.
He is worthy of my praise, and it is the very act
of praising Him that changes my perspective
and enables me to pray with power.

MARLENE BAGNULL

PRAYER

*Rejoice always, pray continually, give thanks
in all circumstances; for this is God's will for you in Christ Jesus.*

1 THESSALONIANS 5:16–18 NIV

Some people find it difficult to pray, even when they have an immediate need and suspect that the help they desire can only come from God. They don't want to bother God. Then there's the Santa Claus problem: you don't want to make the list too long, or you might not get what you really want. Others just feel unworthy. All these worries are perfectly human, but they all do injustice to God.

God *wants* us to ask for His help and believe He will give it in love. He's not too busy, and the number of prayers He will consider have no limit. When He answers, He does so in perfect love, even when the answer is "not now."

There are no rules about praying. We can pray in church or on the interstate. No fancy words are necessary because God knows what we need before we even ask. God just wants to hear from us.

TONI SORTOR

Lord, don't let prayer intimidate me. You simply want to talk.

There is no question God will duck, no battle
He can't win, no topic He doesn't know.
You can't make Him uncomfortable.
You can't push Him too hard.
So go ahead, hit Him with your best shot.

KARON PHILLIPS GOODMAN

CALL ON GOD

"Call to me and I will answer you. I'll tell you marvelous and wondrous things that you could never figure out on your own."

JEREMIAH 33:3 MSG

Where do you turn when life is going well? How about when life isn't going so well? Many times in scripture, God calls us to look to Him for the answers, for wisdom to deal with people and circumstances, not only when we're in trouble but also when life is good.

James 1:5 tells us that when we ask God for wisdom in anything, He will give it to us, gladly and without reproach. When God told Jeremiah He would restore Israel after a time of testing, He urged Jeremiah to call on Him, and He would answer in ways that would reveal His plan for Israel—in ways that nation couldn't even conceive.

In the same way, God will answer our sincere call for help and restoration, and He will show us "things that [we] could never figure out on [our] own."

MARGIE VAWTER

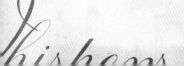

Father, help me to diligently call on You for help, for wisdom.
I know You will give the answers to seemingly impossible questions.

Remember, the shortest distance between a problem
and the solution is the distance between
our knees and the floor.

CHARLES STANLEY

FAULTLESS

To him who is able to keep you from stumbling
and to present you before his glorious presence without fault
and with great joy.

JUDE 24 NIV

Who is at fault? Who is to blame? When something goes wrong at work, at home, or at church, people want to know who made a mistake.

Ever since God confronted Adam and Eve in the Garden of Eden, we have been pointing fingers instead of taking responsibility for our own actions. Shame and fear make us want to deny we have done any wrong, even when we have done so by mistake.

Jesus loves us despite our shortcomings. He is the One who can keep us from falling—who can present us faultless before the Father. Because of this we can have our joy restored no matter what. Whether we have done wrong and denied it or have been falsely accused, we can come into His presence to be restored and lifted up. Let us keep our eyes on Him instead of on our need to justify ourselves to God or others.

NANCY FARRIER

Thank You, Jesus, for Your cleansing love
and for the joy we can find in Your presence.

Often we assume that God is unable to work
in spite of our weaknesses, mistakes, and sins.
We forget that God is a specialist;
He is well able to work our failures
into His plans.

ERWIN LUTZER

More Than an E-mail

*You are a letter from Christ. . .written not with pen and ink
but with the Spirit of the living God.*

2 Corinthians 3:3 nlt

Most of us can't go a day without checking our e-mail.
But don't you just love it when you go to the mailbox,
and stuck between a bunch of bills is a letter? A real
letter is special because the other person took the
time to think about you and went to the trouble to
handwrite a precious note just for you. That beats an
e-mail any day!

We've all heard it said that sometimes we are the only
Bible a person will ever read. We are a letter from Christ.
Try to go the extra mile with people. Be more than an
e-mail: be a precious letter from Christ, and take the
time to let them know how loved and treasured they are
by you and by the Lord!

MariLee Parrish

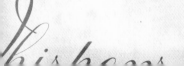

*Father, help me make the people in my life feel loved
and cherished. Help me to remember that I am a letter
from You as I interact with others.*

Our ultimate success totally depends on God:
God's Son the Living Word, and God's written
Word in us, filling us, directing us.

LOIS EVANS

CHILD'S PLAY

*"Unless you change and become like little children,
you will never enter the kingdom of heaven."*

MATTHEW 18:3 NIV

Biographer James Boswell recounted his memory of a boyhood day when his father took him fishing. Boswell gleaned important life lessons from his dad as they sat on the creek bank waiting for a bite on their fishing lines.

Someone checked the journal Boswell's father kept to determine what he recorded about the excursion. The inquirer found one sentence: *Gone fishing today with my son; a day wasted.*

Have you ever felt the same when you played catch with a nephew or took your child to the zoo although you had errands to run?

As our to-do list grows, it becomes harder to engage in child's play. But often we need to enter the world of make-believe, where clocks and adult responsibilities are as extinct as toy dinosaurs.

Spending time with a child affords us the opportunity to influence him or her for God's kingdom. So don't waste another moment; seize the day and play!

TINA KRAUSE

Father, help me to learn to play and enjoy the children You have brought into my life.

Puppies and children are so alike.
They look around their world with amazement.
"Wow! What a place to explore and conquer!"
And they both want to feel safe and secure.

H. NORMAN WRIGHT

PUT ON THE ARMOR

Finally, be strong in the Lord and in his mighty power. Put on the full armor of God, so that you can take your stand against the devil's schemes.

EPHESIANS 6:10–11 NIV

As your relationship with the Lord grows closer, Satan will attempt to knock you off course. Has your soul ever felt oppressed for no particular reason? Satan is powerful and persistent, devising schemes that undermine the Lord's work in our lives. He will go to great lengths to prevent the advancement of God's kingdom on earth.

Don't get discouraged. God has already won the battle! Christ claimed the victory by overcoming death, defeating Satan once and for all. He gives that victory to us.

Put on the spiritual armor Christ provides. We can't fend off Satan's attacks without it. We will triumph over him as we put on the belt of truth, breastplate of righteousness, helmet of salvation, shield of faith, and sword of the Spirit. Don't face your adversary ill prepared. Put on the full armor of God and stand!

JULIE RAYBURN

Dear Lord, remind me to wear the full armor
You have given me to ensure spiritual victory.

No truce while the foe is unconquered;
No laying the armor down!

Fanny Crosby

TRUE LOVE

*Besides that, they learn to be idlers, going about from house
to house, and not only idlers, but also gossips and busybodies,
saying what they should not.*

1 TIMOTHY 5:13 ESV

Scripture connects gossip with idleness, and Paul warns
Christians against engaging in it.

Those who care deeply about their families may
encourage, praise, or defend them; but they do not
gossip, because they know the damage this causes
to family relationships. Gossip easily passes from
one person to another, usually because it contains
damaging information or opinions. Our base natures
naturally revel in such things, and Paul did not want us
to encourage ourselves in sin.

That doesn't mean we don't occasionally become
irritated with loved ones and slip up. In the heat of
emotion, we may fail. But a proper Christian
response is to recognize gossip as sin, confess
it, and seek to change.

Then we will truly be loving our
families.

PAMELA L. McQUADE

Lord, keep a guard over my mind and lips.
I don't want to fall to the temptations of gossip.
Help me love my family more than I love a juicy gossip tidbit.

[There is] no surer sign of an unprofitable life
than when people give way to censoriousness
and inquisitiveness into the lives of other men.

FRANCIS DE SALES

Praise or Complain?

I will proclaim the name of the Lord.
Oh, praise the greatness of our God!

DEUTERONOMY 32:3 NIV

Have you ever heard the expression, "Praise and be raised, or complain and remain?" That phrase packs a punch! It means if you complain about your current circumstances, you'll remain there a lot longer than if you'd just praise the Lord in spite of it all.

Sure, that's easy to say, but it's not so easy to do. Praising God during difficult times is the last thing I want to do. I'd rather retreat to my bedroom with a box of Junior Mints and sulk awhile. But sulking won't change things any more than complaining will.

By praising God during the dark times, we're telling God that we trust Him. Anyone can trust God and praise Him on the mountaintop, but only those who really know God's faithfulness can praise Him in the valley. During those valley times, we truly feel God's tender mercy and experience extreme spiritual growth.

So praise God today. Through your praise, you open the door for God to work in your life.

MICHELLE MEDLOCK ADAMS

Lord, help me to resist complaining and praise You instead.

Praise is a contradiction of pride.
Pride says "look at me," but praise longs
for people to see Jesus.

MATT REDMAN

Do the Next Thing

"My food," said Jesus, "is to do the will of him
who sent me and to finish his work."

JOHN 4:34 NIV

Busyness is the curse of modern life. There are enough chores to last a lifetime. Even if you live in a tiny apartment and eat only take-out food, there are still phone calls to make, floors to scrub, and errands to run.

But the Bible says God has numbered our days. He knows how long we have to live, and He knows best what we should do with the time He has given us.

Christian author Elisabeth Elliot gives this advice about how to decide what to do: "Just do the next thing." These simple words echo Jesus' teaching, and in this He is our model. He did nothing that wasn't God's perfect will, and He was perfectly content.

When we feel harried and stressed, it is often because we are trying to do more than God has asked us to do.

God always gives us enough time to do His will.

LAURA FREUDIG

Father, help me see the things I have and want to do,
and order them according to Your will.

Submerge as much of your day as you can,
to make it your invisible keel, by eliminating less
important things. You need time to look into the
face of God, time to read and study his Word
systematically, time to think and plan for your life,
time to praise, time to intercede, time to get
wisdom for handling people and
for making decisions.

ANNE ORTLUND

LISTEN TO HIS VOICE

Now choose life, so that you and your children may live and that you may love the Lord your God, listen to his voice, and hold fast to him.

DEUTERONOMY 30:19–20 NIV

Can you hear the voice of God? Cell phones ringing, MP3 players blasting, high-definition TVs blaring. . . how do we hear God in the middle of all this?

God's voice becomes clear when we pour ourselves into His Word. Take the time to be alone with God, and listen to His voice. What does it sound like? It's unlikely that you will hear a burning bush speak to you, as Moses did. Instead, you will hear Him speak to you through His timeless, authoritative Word.

God speaks to those who are *listening.* In John 10:27, Jesus says for us to listen to His voice. Spend time in God's Word and take time to listen.

MARILEE PARRISH

Dear God, I truly want to hear Your voice.
Please show me how to quiet my life so that
I can know what Your voice sounds like.

God delights in communicating with His people;
therefore, we must seek to increase our ability
to listen to what He is saying.

JANE HAMON

CHANGELESS

"I the Lord do not change."

MALACHI 3:6 NIV

Life doesn't always go the way we expect. Just as everything's running smoothly, the washing machine dies or the furnace stops pumping out heat. The things of this world break down—they change. That includes people, who neglect or harm us or leave our lives. Other days we disappoint ourselves in a big way with our own lack of consistency.

But when situations or people, even ourselves, let us down, we need not despair: God never changes or fails us. Our Lord promised to save us, and He will. Everything in our lives, good or ill, points us toward our heavenly destination; all we face on this side of eternity has a purpose that ends in God's plan. Every changeable situation is designed to bring out holiness in us, though we may not see it as we're hauling dirty clothes to the Laundromat.

Trust your life to the unchangeable One. He will never let you down.

PAMELA L. MCQUADE

Thank You, Lord, for never altering.
Help me trust in You, no matter how often I fail You or myself.

God will be no different tomorrow than
he is today. His love for us is the same.
His power to meet our needs is unchanged.

JIM CYMBALA AND DEAN MERRILL

THE HARDEST
PERSON TO FORGIVE

*This is how we know that we belong to the truth,
and how we set our hearts at rest in his presence: If our hearts condemn us,
we know that God is greater than our hearts, and he knows everything.*

1 JOHN 3:19–20 NIV

Felicia struggled with forgiveness—not in the way you might expect. Felicia loved her friends and family members intensely, forgave them easily, and didn't hold grudges.

But Felicia had trouble forgiving herself. Even after she had confessed her sins to the Lord, she didn't *feel* forgiven. A shadow of guilt constantly hung over her. It was a miserable way to live.

At a retreat, Felicia heard the speaker say, "If God promises something in scripture, and you don't take Him at His word, you're sinning."

The realization hit her like a lightning bolt. *In not receiving forgiveness, I've been sinning even more*, Felicia thought. *Oh Lord, I'm such a mess!*

Then she heard the Lord speak to her heart. *That's okay*, He said. *I love you anyway.*

Right then and there, Felicia chose to believe Him.

DENA DYER

Father God, thank You for Your sweet forgiveness.
Help me forgive others—and myself.

Sometimes the only way to forgive ourselves
is by remembering our humanity.

ROBERT JEFFRESS

A HEAVENLY FATHER

You are my God, and I will praise you;
you are my God, and I will exalt you.

PSALM 118:28 NIV

When I think about my earthly father, I always smile. My dad dotes on his children. My sister teases that she's his favorite, and I tease back that I am, but in all honesty, he makes both of us feel like the favorite child. And if you asked my brother, he'd say *he* was Dad's favorite! That's just how my dad is, and that's exactly how God is, too. He is a doting Dad. He loves us so much. In fact, He adores us!

But I don't love my dad because he is good to me or even because he makes me feel I'm his favorite. I love my dad simply because he is Dad. You know, we should love our heavenly Father simply because He is our Father. That's what Psalm 118:28 says to me: "You are my God, and I will give you thanks." Tell Him today how much you love Him—just for being Him.

MICHELLE MEDLOCK ADAMS

Father, I am so thankful that
You are my heavenly Father.

God's children are God's children anywhere
and everywhere, and shall be even unto the end.
Nothing can sever that sacred tie,
or divide us from his heart.

CHARLES SPURGEON

WHAT'S YOUR FRAGRANCE?

He uses us to spread the knowledge of Christ everywhere,
like a sweet perfume. Our lives are a Christ-like fragrance rising up to God.

2 CORINTHIANS 2:14–15 NLT

The average human being can detect up to ten
thousand different odors. Smells evoke powerful
images—the smell of mothballs takes us right back to
when we were eight years old and playing in Grandma's
attic. The scent of pine transports us to the ski vacation
we took in college.

As followers of Christ, we have been given a very
unique fragrance. And our very presence in the lives of
others always leaves a lingering scent. When we are kind
to someone who doesn't deserve it, it smells wonderful.
When we help a person in need, the fragrance lingers
long after we've gone. Regardless of what we do, our
fragrance should *always* remind people of Christ.

Today, what kind of fragrance do you take with
you? Pause for a moment to ask God to help you be a
sweet representative of Christ, leaving His delightful
aroma lingering in the air behind you.

JOANNA BLOSS

Father, help me to touch, in some small way,
each person I meet today.

When a believer has been steeped in grace,
all the members of his or her immediate
society detect a refreshing fragrance.

CHRISTINE WOOD

NOT MY FAULT!

Hot tempers start fights; a calm, cool spirit keeps the peace.

PROVERBS 15:18 MSG

Does it seem like a sin to be irritable? Irritability certainly can't be compared to murder, stealing, or adultery. Besides, there can be physical reasons as to why we're irritable: lack of sleep or a certain time of the month. It's not our fault! Irritability shouldn't really be classified as a sin. . . .

Or *should* it?

The problem with expressing ourselves in an irritable way is that we don't see it as a sin. We end up tolerating irritability. The truth is that it's wrong. It's hurtful. It starts with a bad commute and a crowded grocery store and the news that the car needs to have new brakes. We walk into a kitchen, find a sink filled with breakfast dishes, and everyone gets a dose of our pent-up frustration.

We need to take irritability seriously, to call it a sin. If we don't, we tolerate it. A better way is to go to God, confess it, and ask for His forgiveness and grace.

SUZANNE WOODS FISHER

Lord, I confess my habit of irritability.
Hold me accountable until this pattern is broken.

If things upset, irritate, or even momentarily bother
me, let me think of what Christ endured
for me and the contrast will put
my troubles in perspective.

ELISABETH ELLIOT

SUFFERING IN SILENCE

*Confess your sins to each other and pray for
each other so that you may be healed.*

JAMES 5:16 NLT

Years ago, Ruth decided the best way to maneuver through
life was to plaster on a smile and go about her day. Inside
her heart, however, she is dying. She has struggles—
addictions. She wishes she could tell another woman who
would listen, but what if she is the only one struggling?

So she remains silent—mostly because she thinks
people will judge her, but also because everyone seems to
be in such a hurry. Sure, her friends mean well, but few
have time to stop to listen to a friend's deepest hurts.

Ruth's story is painful but common—one that
many women experience alone. How can we help?
We can look past the plastered-on smiles. We can ask
questions and actually listen to the answers. We can be
willing to help and pray for someone.

Who knows? A day may come when we are the ones
who need to express the truth and be set free.

KATE E. SCHMELZER

Lord, break through our silence,
and give us compassion for one another.

There is a time to listen, a time to learn,
and a time to do something different,
in the beauty of this silent moment.

DON OSGOOD

SHUT THE DOOR

*"When you pray, go into your room, and when you have
shut your door, pray to your Father who is in the secret place."*

MATTHEW 6:6 NKJV

We all have lists: things to buy, things to do, even a list
for God. *Lord, I want. . . God, I need. . .and if You could please. . .*

He meets your needs because He loves you and
wants to give you His best. Have you ever wondered
what God wants? He wants you—your attention,
affection, praise, and worship. He wants to be
included in your life.

Prayer isn't just a time to give God our list, but a
time to enjoy each other's company. In the busyness
of life, we must be careful that our "quiet time" never
becomes insignificant because it's limited to the needs
we feel we must tell God about. We must remember
our most precious desire—just spending time
with Him.

Shut out the rest of the world, and
discover how little anything else matters
but God.

SHANNA D. GREGOR

Father, forgive me for not taking time to spend with You.
Help me to listen and include You in my life at all times.

Connection with God, which is the reason
for any spiritual practice, begins with changing
our focus (from ourselves and our problems
to God and his sufficiency) and changing
our pace (from hurried and distracted
to deliberate and focused).

KERI WYATT KENT

THE VET'S

The Lord disciplines those he loves.

PROVERBS 3:12 NIV

One of the cats has to go to the vet's today—her ears are itching. I wouldn't mind, if it didn't involve getting her into and out of the cat carrier. Doing so requires qualities only found in the Special Forces: infiltration, encirclement, and neutralization. Then there's the effort required to fold four rigid, outspread legs down into the carrier without being seriously scratched.

Cats are not stupid. They know they will no longer hurt when it's over and we bring them home in about ten minutes. But still they fight. They act as if we were trying to kill them when we are actually saving them.

I'm no better when God decides I am in need of correction or remedy. I fight it every time. Fortunately, God is patient and doesn't use brute force on me. As with the cats when it's time to go home, all He does is leave the door open and I walk right in.

TONI SORTOR

Lord, deep down inside, I know You only want to do me good—
remind me of that when I see that "cat carrier."

The sting of a reproach is the truth of it.

BENJAMIN FRANKLIN

THE WORLD'S FIRST GPS SYSTEM

*The pillar of cloud also moved from in front and stood behind them,
coming between the armies of Egypt and Israel.
Throughout the night the cloud brought darkness to the one side
and light to the other side; so neither went near the other all night long.*

EXODUS 14:19–20 NIV

The world's first known GPS system was the pillar of
cloud by day and fire by night that led the Israelites
through the Sinai Peninsula. Imagine how comforting
it was for the Israelites to follow that pillar on their
trek. It was a visible symbol of the presence of God.

Imagine if we had that holy pillar outside our front
door to help us with big decisions.

We do have that holy pillar outside our homes.
Inside, too. The Bible! Searching God's Word is like
following a map. He shows us where we need to
end up and how we need to get there. The
Bible teaches us to listen for God's directions,
whether it's "Stop!" or "Quick, get a
move on!" God's voice in our ear is the
only map we need.

SUZANNE WOODS FISHER

Lord God, Your Word is better than a holy pillar.

When you know what God says,
what He means, and how to put His truths
into practice, you will be equipped for every
circumstance of life.

KAY ARTHUR

SPEAKING TRUTH

"My mouth speaks what is true, for my lips detest wickedness."

PROVERBS 8:7 NIV

Mary sighed as she hung up the phone. It was her mom—for the third time that day. "Your sister says I'm too involved in your lives," her mother had announced. "*You* don't think that's true, do you?"

Mary hesitated. Her sister was right, but Mary couldn't bear to tell her mother. Instead she said, "Mom, I think you just care very much about us, that's all." As the words left her mouth, Mary felt her face redden. Once again she'd copped out. The truth was that her mother's constant meddling was really starting to take its toll on their relationship.

Telling the truth is often accompanied by consequences. When we are truthful with others, it can sometimes mean hurting their feelings or changing the relationship. But the Bible is clear—when we fail to speak the truth in love, we fail to live authentic lives and can do real damage to ourselves and others.

What steps can you take today to be more truthful?

JOANNA BLOSS

Lord, teach me how to speak truth in love,
even when I am unsure of the outcome.

Change takes place when truth is
presented in relationship.

<small>LARRY CRABB</small>

TOUGH LOVE

Dear children, let's not merely say that we love each other;
let us show the truth by our actions.

1 JOHN 3:18 NLT

The relationship between speech and actions is seen
throughout the Bible. Joseph's brothers *tell* Jacob they are
sad that their brother is dead, yet they staged his death and
sold him into slavery. Pontius Pilate *declares* that he thinks
Jesus is innocent but gives the order to crucify Him. As the
adage goes, "Actions speak louder than words."

We are called to intentionally love one another,
not with meaningless words, but with quantifiable
actions. The command to love actively is much more
difficult than loving with words. Loving with words
requires little thought and no commitment. Loving
with actions requires firm purpose and devotion.

Jesus embodies active love. He loved those
who most thought were unlovable, and in the
ultimate act of love, dying on the cross to save
every one of us from our sin.

First John asks us to love as Jesus
loved. We must push our selfishness
aside and give ourselves fully to others
with active and truthful love.

MANDY NYDEGGER

Dear Lord, teach me to love as You love.

Love has no other message but its own.
Every day we try to live out Christ's love in
a very tangible way in every one of our deeds.
If we do any preaching, it is done with deeds,
not with words.

MOTHER TERESA

REFLECTIONS

"You are precious to me. You are honored, and I love you."

ISAIAH 43:4 NLT

Brenda stood before the bathroom mirror, her fingers clutching a mass of hip flesh. *Humph.* Pinch an inch? This might be *three* inches. She sighed heavily and, with shoulders bent in discouragement, walked out of the bathroom and away from her reflection.

The world would have us believe that we need to be skinny, five feet, eight inches tall, blond, blue-eyed, and amply endowed in the bosom to have any self-worth. That's not the truth. No matter what we look like on the outside, in God's eyes, we are precious. Not only are we precious, but we are honored. And He loves us!

That's not to say we should neglect our appearance. But our confidence and self-worth should not depend on how the world sees us, just on how God sees us: precious, honored, and loved. It doesn't get any better than that.

So the next time you're discouraged with your appearance, check your reflection in God's mirror. You'll be picture perfect!

DONNA K. MALTESE

Lord, my body may not be perfect, but Your love for me is!
Thank You for loving me so very much just as I am!

Shape and height, texture and color are determined
by the amazing genes that the Lord implanted
in you as He designed you in the womb.
These were His gifts to you. Be assured that
God likes what He created you to be,
in all your physical features.
You are beautiful to Him.

PAT WARREN

FLOATING IN GRACE

"Be still, and know that I am God."

PSALM 46:10 NIV

Sometimes we want answers while we are thrashing in the waves of our own doubt, but the truth is, we seldom find wisdom until we are still. When we're tossed about, the horizon may, for the moment, leave our sight. And we are lost. These are the times when we are called to stillness.

Silence and stillness are the doorways that welcome our weary hearts in prayer. Prayer can be full of lamenting and asking, but when we realize that deep prayer is more a quieting of the soul, the power of who God is floods into our hearts. Through this kind of prayer, love rushes in and renews us.

The God who parted the Red Sea and calmed the storms is the same God who works His grace into our everyday lives. Eternity is on the horizon. All we need to do is look to Him, and we will float in depths where our feet can't touch and walk over anything that threatens to overcome us.

SARAH HAWKINS

Father, help me begin every day in prayer,
that I may have a better understanding of You.

Whether we feast through silence, through stillness,
through meditation or contemplation,
God longs to feed us.

<small>JANE RUBIETTA</small>

REAL INVINCIBILITY

I can do all this through him who gives me strength.

PHILIPPIANS 4:13 NIV

Remember that powerful song "I Am Woman" performed by Helen Reddy? I remember my mother belting out: "I am strong. I am invincible. I am WOMAN!"

She sang with such passion. I didn't understand that emotion then, but I certainly understand it now. Aren't those empowering words?

Some days I feel more like singing, "I'm a worm on the floor." How about you? Do you ever feel less than powerful?

I've got good news, and it's even better than Helen Reddy's song. God's Word says that we can do *all* things through Christ who gives us strength. All means *all*, right? So no matter how you feel today, you can accomplish whatever is on your plate.

See, you don't have to *feel* powerful to *be* powerful. The God in you is all-powerful, and He will cause you to triumph. After all, you are more than a woman— you are a child of the Most High God. Now that's something to sing about!

MICHELLE MEDLOCK ADAMS

Thank You, Lord, that even when I feel powerless,
You are powerful. Help me to be courageous for You.

Nothing transcends the power of God.
Whether our difficulty is from Satan, others,
self-inflicted, or experienced in the process of
our obedience, it is God's prerogative to rearrange,
reconstruct, reinterpret, and realign the situation
to bring glory and praise to His name.

JOSEPH STOWELL

HOSPITALITY AND FRIENDSHIP

Cheerfully share your home with
those who need a meal or a place to stay.

1 PETER 4:9 NLT

When Anne was young, having company meant
frenetically cleaning the house from floor to ceiling,
shopping for groceries, and cooking elaborate meals.
Company meant trying to make a good impression.

After several years of anxious entertaining, Anne
heard her mentor say she did not worry what the house
looked like when company came over. All that mattered
was that people would come as they were and she would
receive them as she was. Anne's mentor focused solely
on *ministering* to her guests.

Shortly after this discussion, Anne had ten women
coming to her home, and she barely had time to cook
or shop. Instead of panicking, she simply cleaned
the bathrooms and kitchen where cleaning really
counted. Instead of planning elaborate meals, she
prepared a simple breakfast. And instead of
cooking lunch, she had a simple, hearty
meal delivered by a local restaurant. The
day could not have gone better, and Anne
relaxed and enjoyed it as well.

JUNE HETZEL, PHD

*Lord, help me focus on relationships
and cultivate authentic friendships.*

When we are willing to open our homes,
our kitchens, our living rooms,
and most of all our hearts to others,
God can make exciting things happen.

RACHAEL CRABB AND RAEANN HART

SIMPLY IRRESISTIBLE

Love never fails.

1 CORINTHIANS 13:8 NIV

If you found out you could become simply irresistible, wouldn't you want to know how? If the ability to become irresistible came in a bottle, wouldn't you rush to the store to buy it? Women pay millions of dollars every year on beauty products and cosmetic surgery to look better. It seems we'd all like to be irresistible.

The advertising executives know this, which is why they call perfumes "Very Irresistible" and other similar names. They know women desire that irresistible quality and they'll pay almost anything to achieve it.

Well, search no more. I have the secret to being irresistible, and you can't get it in a bottle or a potion of any kind. You can't buy it. You'll only find it in the Bible. God's love makes us irresistible. The more you have inside you, the more irresistible you'll become.

See, people are drawn to the love of God. They long for it. And God's love never fails. Read 1 Corinthians 13 today, and ask the Lord to fill you with His love. Soon, you'll be absolutely irresistible.

MICHELLE MEDLOCK ADAMS

Lord, I know You are irresistible. Help me share Your love.

The beautiful thing about God's love is that it is a giving love—a love that flows in abundance with kindness, generosity, and goodness.

ROY LESSIN

BURDEN BEARING

The heartfelt counsel of a friend
is as sweet as perfume and incense.

PROVERBS 27:9 NLT

Janet's friends and family often came to her for advice. She always seemed to have just the right words to say. Lately, though, she was feeling overwhelmed because it seemed like everyone needed her at once. Besides, she had her own problems and responsibilities. What she really wanted was some time away—from her loved ones *and* their problems.

Caring for others and offering wise counsel is biblical. God created us to live in community, and we are instructed to bear one another's burdens. But there is often a fine line between bearing others' burdens and bearing *responsibility* for their burdens. It drains us, and it can keep them from seeking answers directly from God.

Our job is to point others to Christ, not become a substitute for Him. Allowing our friends unlimited access to our advice and counsel is one way this can happen. Sometimes the wisest words of advice we can offer are "Tell it to Jesus."

JOANNA BLOSS

Father, help me discern the difference between bearing others'
burdens and taking responsibility for their problems.
Help me to point others to You.

If you find yourself trying to rescue your
friend or loved one, then ask God
to help you let go of the burden.
Rescue is not ultimately your responsibility;
it is God's.

RUTH GRAHAM AND STACY MATTINGLY

GOD'S PICKET FENCE

The name of the LORD is a strong tower; the righteous runs into it and is safe.

PROVERBS 18:10 NASB

It's a dangerous world. Drunk drivers, heart attacks, unemployment, terrorism. . . It is easy to think about all the bad things that could happen. But Jesus says: "Do not worry" (Matthew 6:31 NASB).

Worry shows our lack of trust in God's love and power. The Bible is as clear about God's promises of protection for those who love Him as it is about the injunction not to worry. In fact, one necessarily follows the other: we shouldn't worry *because* God is taking care of us. The Bible says that we can rejoice; we can spend our days singing praise to God, knowing that His protection is all around us.

We don't always have fences around our houses, and even if we did, they couldn't protect our families from everything. But we do have a promise from God that He stands eternal sentry over those who love Him.

LAURA FREUDIG

Dear Lord, I praise You for Your immense power,
Your love, and Your faithfulness.
Forgive me for worrying and help me trust in Your promises.

Concern draws us to God.
Worry pulls us from him.

JOANNA WEAVER

MALLS

But godliness with contentment is great gain.
For we brought nothing into the world, and we can take nothing out of it.

1 TIMOTHY 6:6–7 NIV

Our area has first-class shopping malls, complete with restaurants, rides for kids, and theaters. I hate them all. I can spend hours wandering a mall here and never find what I need. It's easier to go downtown and not find what I need.

Yet when we're on vacation, I love malls. They fill up a rainy day and give some indication of the spirit of the area. I especially love malls without a single "designer" store but two or three outdoor supply stores carrying rough woolen jackets, rain gear that keeps you 100 percent dry, and locally made leather shoes.

These malls are small and friendly. The bookstores are full of good mysteries and local lore. The clerks go out of their way to be helpful; the shoppers smile a lot. But I bet the residents of that vacation area hate their own malls and can't wait to visit mine. The cement is always grayer on the other side of the fence, you see.

TONI SORTOR

Lord, give me contentment, no matter where I am.

God warns us that seeking our own brand of
contentment apart from Him is futile,
for "the bed is too short to stretch out on,
the blanket too narrow to wrap around you."

MARSHA CROCKETT

WORKS OF DARKNESS

*And have no fellowship with the unfruitful works of darkness,
but rather reprove them.*

EPHESIANS 5:11 KJV

Have you ever known Christians who adopt worldly standards to attract friends? Popularity ranks higher on their list of priorities than bringing people to the Savior.

Some try to combine questionable or blatantly sinful activities with some form of religion, with the excuse that it's their way of reaching people for Christ. This hinders their witness, and the unsaved still don't trust Christ.

Paul calls this "fellowship with the unfruitful works of darkness." He says we must have no part of it. Making people comfortable in their sin is nothing more than facilitating their rejection of Christ. No favors are done by encouraging any sinful lifestyles. All that does is to make people comfortable on the way to eternity separated from God.

There just is no fellowship between godliness and worldliness. God calls us to avoid the darkness in the world. Jesus asks us to reach out to others in His name through prayer and God's Word—not by lowering our standards.

RACHEL QUILLIN

*Father, help me to base my standards on
Your Word and not let the world infiltrate my life.*

You are called not to be successful or to meet any of
the other counterfeit standards of this world,
but to be faithful and to be expended in the cause of
serving the risen and returning Christ.

CHARLES COLSON

SAY WHAT?

Don't fool yourself into thinking that you are a listener when you are anything but, letting the Word go in one ear and out the other. Act on what you hear!

JAMES 1:22 MSG

Have you ever tried to talk to someone who is engrossed in a television show? "Yeah, I'm listening," the person replies in a less-than-attentive voice.

James seems to be in a similar situation, frustrated by those who pretend to listen and yet do not apply what they have heard.

So often we find ourselves tuning out the minister on Sunday morning. We look up at the end of a sermon and don't know what we've heard. We pretend to hear, but we are really letting the Word of God go in one ear and out the other.

Our minds must be disciplined to really listen to God's Word. Then we must do the more difficult thing—*act* on what we've heard.

MANDY NYDEGGER

Dear Lord, please teach me to be attentive to Your Word.
Help me to act on the things You teach me
so that mine becomes a practical faith.

Christian love is practical;
it doesn't just say words,
it does what needs to be done.

WARREN WIERSBE

QUICK AND SLOW

My dear brothers and sisters, take note of this:
Everyone should be quick to listen, slow to speak and slow to become angry,
because human anger does not produce the righteousness that God desires.

JAMES 1:19–20 NIV

Kindergartners learning traffic signals know that yellow means "slow down." James 1:19–20 also is a yellow light!

Have you wished, after a conversation with a friend, that you had not given that unsolicited advice? Your friend needed a listening ear, but you attempted to fix her problem. Have you raced through a hectic day, only to end it by taking out your frustrations on family members or friends?

Too often words escape before we know what we are saying. Like toothpaste that cannot be put back in the tube, once words are spoken, it is impossible to take them back. Words have a lasting impact.

Practice being quick and slow today—quick to listen, slow to speak, slow to become angry.

EMILY BIGGERS

God, grant me the patience, wisdom,
and grace I need to be a good listener.
Remind me also, Father, to use my words today
to lift others up rather than to tear them down.

Listening means that you're trying to understand
the feelings of the other person and are listening
for his or her sake. This is helping.

H. NORMAN WRIGHT

CAN GOD INTERRUPT YOU?

In their hearts humans plan their course,
but the Lord establishes their steps.

PROVERBS 16:9 NIV

Before rushing out of the house each morning, we grab calendars or PalmPilots. Our day is efficiently planned. We are eager to check off our to-do list. But wait! The phone suddenly rings. There is an unexpected knock at the door. The car tire is flat.

How do we react when our plans are interrupted? Do frustration, resentment, and anger quickly surface?

Perhaps God ordained our interruptions. A friend could be calling in need of encouragement. God knew you'd be just the right person to lift her spirits. Maybe the knock on the door is a lost child seeking help. Perhaps, just perhaps, God may be trying to get your attention.

There is nothing wrong with planning your day. However, God sees the big picture. Be open. Be flexible. Allow God to change your plans in order to accomplish His divine purposes. Instead of becoming frustrated, be willing to join Him. When you do, interruptions will become blessings.

JULIE RAYBURN

Dear Lord, give me Your eternal perspective
so that I may be open to divine interruptions.

It is possible that what we see as an
inconvenient interruption is
a divine appointment.

JOHN ORTBERG

New Every Morning

Because of the Lord's great love we are not consumed,
for his compassions never fail. They are new every morning;
great is your faithfulness.

LAMENTATIONS 3:22–23 NIV

What's the first thing you do when you get up in the morning? Hop on the treadmill? Walk blindly to the bathroom, not opening your eyes until a jet of hot water jolts you awake?

God starts out His day offering renewed compassion to His children. No matter what trials, difficulties, and sins yesterday brought, the morning ushers in a brand-new beginning for believers who seek His forgiveness. All you have to do is accept the gift.

Are you burdened from yesterday's stress? Are the worries of tomorrow keeping you awake at night? Consider the dawning of the day as an opportunity to begin anew with our heavenly Father. Seek Him in the morning through studying His Word and through prayer, embracing His compassion.

ANNIE TIPTON

Father, I never want to take for granted the grace You offer every day. I'm so undeserving, but still You give and give and give. Please help me to show mercy to others the same way You do to me.

God wants you to experience his grace whether you have faced your life with courage or with cowardice. Grace is not about us; it is about God. He will meet you wherever you are to help you take the next gutsy step.

PATSY CLAIRMONT AND TRACI MULLINS

THUNDERSTORM

"How faint the whisper we hear of him!
Who then can understand the thunder of his power?"

JOB 26:14 NIV

When I was young, my father would wake me up and lead me to the porch to watch thunderstorms. He never said much beyond, "Don't worry. It's safe here," but that was enough to ease my fears and enable me to enjoy the wildness spreading out before us and tearing at our hair. Most of the time, we simply stood there in silence and let the glory roll over us.

My father was not a religious man, but he understood power and glory. He called it nature. I accepted that, but knew it was somehow more than nature. We didn't argue about religion, though. I couldn't change his mind, and he allowed me the dignity of my own beliefs.

There weren't many things we agreed on as I grew up, but every time a thunderstorm rolled in, we'd meet on the front porch, and laugh as thunder shook us to the bone and the lightning made spots dance in our eyes. Whatever we attributed it to, it was one awesome light show!

TONI SORTOR

May Your power, Lord, envelop me today.

Storms can be God's messengers.

ANNE GRAHAM LOTZ

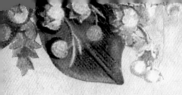

CRISIS COUNSELOR

Offer unto God thanksgiving; and pay thy vows unto the most High:
And call upon me in the day of trouble: I will deliver thee,
and thou shalt glorify me.

PSALM 50:14–15 KJV

We all experience moments of panic when we are almost overwhelmed with the need to talk to someone. The pain is often so great that the only relief we can think of comes through sharing with someone we love or a confidant we feel can help us.

Often the person we want to talk to is not available. Discouragement or depression can result.

God is always there. He never sleeps; He's on call twenty-four hours a day, seven days a week. He is willing not only to listen but to give wise counsel. He gives peace beyond our understanding and joy in the midst of trials.

The next time you find yourself hurting or in a panic, call on God. Ask Him to listen and help you. You'll find He is the only Counselor you need.

NANCY FARRIER

Thank You, Lord, for being there whenever I need You.
Help me to learn to rely on You.

You get to know God real good when He's all ya' got.

JOYCE MEYER

BAD COMPANY

Do not be misled: "Bad company corrupts good character."

1 CORINTHIANS 15:33 NIV

The young nurse began her career with stars in her eyes. However, her naive bubble quickly burst during her first lunch break. Other nurses gossiped viciously about coworkers and then pretended to be best friends on the floor. She vowed to avoid the gossip. But as the weeks passed, she began chiming in during similar conversations. What was happening to her?

We are like sponges, absorbing the contents of our environment. Others influence us—for better or for worse. For that reason, we must choose our friends wisely. Decide what kind of person you would like to become. Spend time with people who exhibit those qualities. Good character produces good character. The opposite is also true.

Bad character is contagious. It is subtle. It doesn't happen overnight. Choose to surround yourself with positive role models that foster good character.

JULIE RAYBURN

Dear Lord, help me choose my friends wisely
so that I will be positively influenced.

A person is made better or worse by his friends.

MABEL HALE

Deluged in Love

Show me the wonders of your great love.

Do you have the kind of love that overflows to everyone around you?

A firefighter at our church recently shared with us that firefighters use a piece of equipment called a deluge nozzle for really big fires. This nozzle puts out fifteen hundred gallons of water per minute. Now that's a lot of water!

Wouldn't it be neat if they could invent a deluge love nozzle, guaranteed to put out fifteen hundred gallons of love per minute? Then each time I feel impatience, irritability, or frustration rising up inside of me, I could just reach for the deluge love nozzle and spew some love around.

There may not be a deluge love nozzle in existence, but we have something even better—Jesus Christ, our secret weapon of love. He can cause you to spew more love than even a deluge nozzle. So call on Him today. He's got enough love to totally soak your family.

MICHELLE MEDLOCK ADAMS

Lord, thank You for being my secret love weapon.
Help me to share Your love today.

When we are experiencing ourselves as the beloved of
God, accepted and cherished by Him in all our beauty
and brokenness, our hard, rough edges start to soften.
We begin to see others as beloved as well,
and that is what gets reflected back to them when they
look into our eyes. Not only does the love of God
come to us in solitude, the love of God begins
to pour through us to others.

Ruth Haley Barton

COMFORT FOOD

For whatever things were written before were written
for our learning, that we through the patience
and comfort of the Scriptures might have hope.

ROMANS 15:4 NKJV

A big mound of ice cream topped with hot fudge, grilled cheese sandwiches and warm chicken noodle soup fixed by Mom—comfort food. Those comfort foods soothe the body and mind because they remind us of happier and more secure times.

Romans 15:4 tells us the scriptures are comfort food for the soul. They were written and given so that, through our learning, we would be comforted with the truths of God. Worldly pleasures bring temporary comfort. However, the words of God are soothing and provide permanent hope and peace. Through God's Word, you will be changed, and your troubles will dim in the bright light of Christ.

So the next time you are sad, lonely, or disappointed, before you turn to pizza, turn to the Word of God as your source of comfort.

NICOLE O'DELL

Thank You, Father,
for the rich comfort Your Word provides.

The holy scripture is the highest
and best of books, abounding in comfort
under all afflictions and trials.

MARTIN LUTHER

ONE DAY AT A TIME

Blessed be the Lord, who daily loadeth us with benefits,
even the God of our salvation.

PSALM 68:19 KJV

There's a reason why the Lord's Prayer teaches us to ask for daily bread. God calls us to a childlike faith that basks in the provisions of the moment.

Think about small children. A toddler may cry when another child knocks him down and takes away his ball. The tears disappear when his mother hugs him and gives him a kiss. He lives in the moment.

God always provides for us. Benefits overflow the shopping carts of our lives every single day. But He only gives us what we need for today, not for tomorrow. By tomorrow, even later today, we may forget all that God has done for us. The Bible verse that spoke to us this morning feels empty by afternoon.

God gives us blessings every day so that we still have what we need after we have spent ourselves on life's disappointments.

DARLENE FRANKLIN

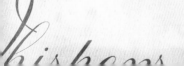

Father, You give us bread daily. We praise You
for Your constant care and ask that You will train
our eyes to focus on Your blessings.

All of my need He freely supplieth,
Day after day His goodness I prove;
Mercies unfailing, new every morning,
Tell me of God's unchangeable love.

THOMAS CHISHOLM

FAITH, THE EMOTIONAL BALANCER

*No man is justified by the law in the sight of God,
it is evident: for, The just shall live by faith.*

GALATIANS 3:11 KJV

Our moods often dictate our actions. For instance, we schedule lunch with a friend for Saturday afternoon, but on Saturday morning we regret having made plans. Or we strategize what to accomplish on our day off but suffer from mental anemia and physical fatigue when the day arrives. So we fail to do what we had intended to do in a more enthusiastic moment.

Emotions mislead us. The emotional roller coaster thrusts us into mood changes and affects what we do, what we say, and the attitudes that define us.

It has been said that faith is the bird that feels the light and sings to greet the dawn while it is still dark. The Bible instructs us to live by faith—not by feelings. Faith assures us that daylight will dawn in our darkest moments, affirming God's presence so that even when we fail to pray and positive feelings fade, our moods surrender to song.

TINA KRAUSE

Heavenly Father, I desire for my faith,
not my emotions, to dictate my life.

Faith includes noticing the mess,
the emptiness and discomfort,
and letting it be there until some light returns.

ANNE LAMOTT

ANGER AND
RECONCILIATION

Be ye angry, and sin not: let not the sun go down upon your wrath:
Neither give place to the devil.

EPHESIANS 4:26–27 KJV

Renee lived with anger that permeated all her relationships. Many did not want to be around Renee, for without warning, they often became the recipients of her wrath.

God tells us it is okay to be angry, but we are not to sin. The words "let not the sun go down upon your wrath," mean we are not to let a great deal of time go by before we reconcile. When we don't quickly resolve conflict, our anger festers and we become embittered. We end up allowing Satan a foothold in our lives. The unresolved anger will poison us and destroy relationships with others, leaving us lonely, afflicted, and alone in our wrath.

Surrender your anger to the Lord, asking the Holy Spirit to empower you to forgive and be reconciled to the offender. In this liberation, enjoy the abundant life Jesus came to give us (John 10:10).

TINA C. ELACQUA, PhD

Forgiving Lord, I surrender my anger to You.
Please give me a spirit of reconciliation and the
opportunity to make amends with the offender.

Forgiveness restores the unraveled seam of love
and irons out the wrinkles of residual anger.

EVERETT WORTHINGTON

TEACHER

Even as fools walk along the road,
they lack sense and show everyone how stupid they are.

ECCLESIASTES 10:3 NIV

It wasn't until I tried teaching that I truly came to admire teachers. I was the worst teacher I ever met, a world-class incompetent, so I quit before anyone got wise and fired me. The kids and I had a great time, but I doubt they learned anything useful. Certainly they learned nothing in the curriculum.

I had never taken an education course in college, and I had no intention of becoming a teacher until someone offered me the job. I spent most of that semester just trying to keep order in the classroom. They were good kids; I was a terrible teacher.

But I learned a lot. That semester was my first education in failure. What appeared to be an easy job with good hours was in no way easy. It was a good lesson in humility for a new college graduate who believed a degree could open any door. It might open doors, but it didn't guarantee success—especially when I chose the wrong door to open.

TONI SORTOR

Lead me, Lord, to the right doors in my life.

Humility is not so much a grace
or virtue along with others; it is the root of all,
because it alone assumes the right attitude
before God and allows Him as God to do all.

ANDREW MURRAY

Keeping
a Clean Heart

Beloved, let us cleanse ourselves from all filthiness of the flesh and spirit,
perfecting holiness in the fear of God.

2 Corinthians 7:1 nkjv

Her new home had white ceramic tile floors
throughout. Friends and family often asked, "Won't
they show every speck of dirt?"

"Yes, but at least I can tell if I need to clean them,"
replied the new homeowner.

"So how often do you have to clean them—once a
week?" her friends asked.

"More like every day," she replied, laughing at
their horrified faces.

Keeping a clean heart requires similar diligence
and regular upkeep. While Jesus cleanses us from all
unrighteousness, we need to be on the lookout for
temptations and situations that might cause us to fall
into sin. Reading the Bible reminds us that God expects
us to strive for holiness. As we pray daily, God shows us
areas in our character or behaviors that displease Him.

Like the homeowner who enjoyed knowing her
floors were clean, there is joy and peace knowing our
hearts can be clean, too.

Austine Keller

*"Create in me a clean heart, O God,
and renew a steadfast spirit within me."*

Are you washed in the blood,
In the soul-cleansing blood of the Lamb?

ELISHA HOFFMAN

PERFECTION

Strive for full restoration, encourage one another,
be of one mind, live in peace.
And the God of love and peace will be with you.

2 CORINTHIANS 13:11 NIV

Dictionary.com defines *perfection*:

perfection (per-fek-shuhn) *n.* The quality or
condition of being perfect. The act or process of
perfecting. A person or thing considered to be perfect.
An instance of excellence.

Wow. If I am supposed to be "excellent" all the
time, I'm in a heap of trouble. Some days I might earn
that "Blue Ribbon of Excellence," but lots of days I
wouldn't even qualify for an honorable mention. How
about you?

That's why I like the Christian definition of
perfection a lot better. One inspirational author
defines "Christian perfection" like this:
"loving God with all our heart, mind,
soul, and strength."

Now that seems more doable. If my
heart is right and if I'm truly seeking

God, I can walk in Christian perfection.
And, guess what? You can, too! We may
never win another blue ribbon, but we can
still be winners. Who says nobody's perfect?
If we're in love with God, we are!

MICHELLE MEDLOCK ADAMS

Father, help me to attain Christian perfection every day of my life.

Those who put themselves in His hands will become
perfect, as He is perfect—perfect in love,
wisdom, joy, beauty, and immortality.
The change will not be completed in this life,
for death is an important part of the treatment.

C. S. LEWIS

GOD REJOICES
in Your Confidence

I rejoice therefore that I have confidence in you in all things.

2 CORINTHIANS 7:16 KJV

"But God wants you to have confidence!"

Those words echoed in my head. But stage fright made my palms sweat and my knees quiver. I remembered words of support from a spiritual mentor.

"I don't know if I can do this."

Ann laughed. "But this is an opportunity from God to give your testimony."

"What kind of testimony will it be if I make a fool out of myself?"

"You won't. Pray about it. He gave you the story. He'll certainly give you the confidence to share it."

I heard the hostess winding up her introduction. "Okay, God," I whispered, "let's get me through this and we'll both rejoice." My voice trembled, but as my message began to flow, I relaxed.

God got me through it, of course. God *wants* us to be confident, and He rejoices when our trust in Him gives us the confidence to tackle whatever challenge He puts before us.

RAMONA RICHARDS

Lord, make me confident—in You.

We can become women of confidence
only as we grasp a great view of God.

Pam Farrel

GOD'S WORKMANSHIP

For we are God's handiwork, created in Christ Jesus to do good works,
which God prepared in advance for us to do.

EPHESIANS 2:10 NIV

I've always loved this scripture. Did you know that the word *workmanship* indicates an ongoing process? So, if we are God's workmanship, we are God's ongoing project. In other words, He isn't finished with us yet! Isn't that good news? I am so glad! I'd hate to think that I was as good as I was going to get.

So, if you are feeling less than adequate today—cheer up! God is not through with you yet! He is working on you right now—even as you're reading this devotional. He knew that we'd all make big mistakes, but this scripture says that He created us in Christ Jesus to do good works. He's prepared the road for us. He's been planning our steps long before we arrived here, so don't worry!

We may not be where we want to be today, but we're on the right road. After all, we're God's workmanship, and He only turns out good stuff!

MICHELLE MEDLOCK ADAMS

Thank You, God, for working on me,
perfecting me from glory to glory.

By faith we accept Christ Jesus as our only hope and
Savior. He comes, in Spirit, to live in our heart,
soul, and mind to do the work of re-creating.
By this work of re-creation, God begins to
fashion us into His likeness, His workmanship,
His treasure, His masterpiece.

ANGELA THOMAS MCGUFFEY

GOD'S CURE FOR DISAPPOINTMENT

A man has joy in an apt answer, and how delightful is a timely word!

PROVERBS 15:23 NASB

Hurts often are soothed with the rich love found in our relationships with others. When a friend faces disappointment, we naturally want to make it better for her. A wonderful way to do that is to offer comfort—an understanding smile, a warm hug, or a few words of affirmation.

Comfort is not counsel. A friend may not be looking to us to solve the problem or offer advice. She may simply need a shoulder to cry on, a hand to hold, and a heart that desires to understand. She is looking for a strong spiritual relationship in friends she can trust.

Comfort is God's cure for disappointment. Maybe we don't understand exactly what a friend is going through, but we can offer comfort by being honest—letting her know we have never experienced her situation, but we are there to walk with her through the storm and hold her up when she feels weak.

NICOLE O'DELL

*Lord, help me to be aware of the needs of others
and find the words to reach out to them.*

Personal meaning and human value arise
only in relationship. Solitude casts doubt on them.

Walter Wangerin Jr.

Steadfast Love

Give thanks to the Lord, for he is good; his love endures forever.

PSALM 107:1 NIV

When the sea of life batters us, it's easy to forget the Lord's goodness. Caught up in storms, tunnel vision afflicts us as we view the troubles before us. We may even doubt the Lord, whom we serve. Though we might not consciously separate ourselves from Him, deep inside we fear He won't act to save us—or that He won't act in time.

That's a good time to stop and give thanks to God, who never stops being good or ends His love for us. Our situations change, our love fails, but God never varies. He has not changed, and our doubts cannot make alteration in Him. If we allow faith to take control, we will realize that and turn again to Him.

Facing troubles? Give thanks to the Lord. He is good. He hasn't deserted you, no matter what you face, and His goodness will never end.

PAMELA L. McQUADE

Thank You, Lord, that Your love never changes.
I can depend on it, though my life seems to be crashing around me.
Nothing is larger than You.

Gratitude is the attitude that sets
the altitude for living.

James MacDonald

CONFIDENCE
TO SPEAK THE WORD

"Now, Lord, look on their threats, and grant to Your servants that with all boldness they may speak Your word."

ACTS 4:29 NKJV

Evangelism is not one of my gifts. I've known that for a long time. I'm a writer, a teacher, sometimes a speaker. Yet speaking about those blessings has never been easy for me.

Many of my friends are not Christians. Some of them live rather wild, undisciplined—and often lost—lives. They know I'm a Christian. Yet I'm well aware that they don't want to hear about God and His Son.

When I found this passage, I turned instead to prayer: *Give me the strength to speak of You, Lord—and even more, the right doors.*

The answer I received was this: live it. When I do, my friends feel more comfortable asking me questions about my faith.

Perhaps I'm never meant to reach thousands with my faith. But through this prayer, I've found the confidence to reach out, one friend at a time.

RAMONA RICHARDS

Help me live confidently for You, Lord.

The life-saving strategy of Jesus is based
on ordinary people showing and telling
about Him in ordinary places.

RON HUTCHCRAFT

Good News of Great Joy

"This will be a sign to you:
You will find a baby wrapped in cloths and lying in a manger."

LUKE 2:12 NIV

On December 24, half the town was standing in the checkout lines at the food store, three-quarters of us in a foul mood. Why did the store put in a baffling new credit-card system the week before Christmas? For five sweet potatoes, I would stand in line at least ten minutes. Bah, humbug!

Ahead of me, a tiny baby reclined in his carrier. He was so bundled up his cheeks glowed red. When his eyes met mine, he broke into a full-body smile, feet thrashing merrily, his mouth making little baby gurgles. "He's so beautiful," I told his mother.

In seconds people from neighboring lines were playing peekaboo, smiling at those near them, captivated by the baby's unconditional happiness. Suddenly I knew how the shepherds and wise men felt. "Merry Christmas," I said to the cashier.

"Merry Christmas to you," she replied, still grinning in the baby's direction. "Cash or charge?"

TONI SORTOR

Help me have joy, Lord, in your season.

The right way to penetrate every divine truth,
to enjoy its full relish, and to imprint it
on the heart, is to dwell upon it whilst
its savor continues.

MADAME JEAN GUYON

JUST HALF A CUP

"I am coming to you now, but I say these things while I am still in the world, so that they may have the full measure of my joy within them."

JOHN 17:13 NIV

"Just half a cup, please."

A friend is offered a cup of piping hot coffee, but she declines a full cup. It is difficult and unnatural for her friend to stop pouring at half a cup, so she pours just a bit more, to give her friend the fullest possible measure of enjoyment in that one cup of coffee.

That's how our Father feels when He longs to bestow His richest blessings and wisdom on us. He loves us, so He desires to fill our cup to overflowing. Do you tell Him to stop pouring when your cup is half full? Perhaps your actions dictate that your cup remains half empty. Seek a full cup and enjoy the full measure of the joy of the Lord.

NICOLE O'DELL

*Dear Jesus, forgive me for not accepting the fullness
of Your blessings and Your joy. Help me to see the ways that
I prevent my cup from being filled to overflowing.*

God singles out the humble soul to fill him to the brim
with grace, when the proud is sent away empty.

THOMAS BROOKS

CHANGE IN PERSPECTIVE

Jesus answered, "I am the way and the truth and the life."

JOHN 14:6 NIV

Do you ever get lost? I am what you might call "directionally challenged." It seems that no matter how I try, I get lost on a regular basis. Of course, in my defense, Texas *is* a big place, and you can never return the same way you arrived. It's never a matter of simply reversing the directions.

Getting lost used to really frustrate and frighten me. Now, I consider it more of a fun adventure. I find that something good usually comes from it. For example, recently when I lost my way, I discovered this great garden shop with the most beautiful iron bench. Now that bench adorns our yard—it was meant to be!

It's all in the perspective. I no longer worry when I'm lost. I just enjoy the journey. Life is the same way. There's no sense worrying your way through each day—just enjoy the trip.

After all, if we know Jesus as our Lord and Savior, we're on the right road because He is the Way!

MICHELLE MEDLOCK ADAMS

Thank You, God, for guiding my every step.

Because of the Holy Spirit's witness and illumination,
you never have to be alone in your decisions—
but this is true only as long as you're seeking
the mind of God and wanting to do His will.

TONY EVANS

WHO'S ON THE THRONE?

When Jesus heard this, he said to him, "You still lack one thing.
Sell everything you have and give to the poor,
and you will have treasure in heaven.
Then come, follow me."

LUKE 18:22 NIV

When the rich young ruler approached Jesus, he was
sure he'd covered all the bases. The young man knew
the law and had followed it to the letter since he was a
boy. However, Jesus threw him a curveball.

"All this stuff you love," Jesus said, "get rid of it.
Then follow Me." Jesus' candid answer made the young
man very sad because he had great wealth. Who was
Jesus to ask him to give it all away?

Scripture tells us that anything in our lives that we
put in place of Christ is idolatry. We are far too easily
pleased by the things that many people value and envy
in others.

Is there anything in your life that is taking the
place of Jesus? The cost of following Him is high,
but the rewards are eternal and far too wonderful for
words.

JOANNA BLOSS

216

*Father, help me to put You before everything
I have and everything I do.*

Following God is always the best choice.
It is the safest choice, although it feels anything
but safe in the chaos of change.

MARY ANN FROEHLICH

AUTHOR INDEX

SUZANNE WOODS FISHER wrote the historical novel Copper Star and its sequel, Copper Fire, which were inspired by true events. Fisher also writes for many magazines. She is a wife, mother, and puppy-raiser for Guide Dogs for the Blind. Pages 84, 138, 146

DARLENE FRANKLIN lives in Oklahoma. She is the author of Romanian Rhapsody and the Dressed for Death mystery series, as well as numerous articles. You may visit her at www.darlenefranklinwrites.blogspot.com. Page 188

LAURA FREUDIG has lived most of her life on islands along the Maine coast. She enjoys reading, hiking, and singing with her husband and children. Pages 126, 164

ANNA GINDLESPERGER, a Pittsburgh native, graduated from Milligan College with a bachelor's degree in English. She has pursued a master's in professional writing at Carnegie Mellon University. Page 16

SHANNA D. GREGOR is a freelance writer, editor, and product developer. The mother of two young men, Shanna resides in Tucson, Arizona, with her husband. Pages 26, 38, 74, 142

JENNIFER HAHN is a freelance writer, compiler, and proof-reader who lives in Pennsylvania's Amish country. She and her husband, Mark, have two daughters and a son. Page 64

SARAH HAWKINS is an English and Bible teacher to junior high students and has often taught a women's Bible study. She lives with her husband and son in Northern California. Pages 106, 154

JUNE HETZEL, PhD, is professor of education at Biola University. She enjoys the roles of wife, friend, author, editor, and professor. She and her husband, Geoff, reside in Southern California. Page 158

AUSTINE KELLER resides in Tampa, Florida, writing and publishing as a ministry to others as well as for her own enjoyment. She also enjoys a newly emptied nest and fishing with her husband. Page 196

TINA KRAUSE is an award-winning newspaper columnist and author of the book Laughter Therapy. She is a wife, mom, and grandmother of four. Tina and her husband, Jim, live in Valparaiso, Indiana. Pages 118, 190

P. J. LEHMAN lives in Valrico, Florida, with her husband and three children. She enjoys children's ministry, photography, animals, being outdoors, and—her all-time favorite—a hammock with a good book! Pages 28, 72, 92

DONNA K. MALTESE is a writer, editor, and the author of Power Prayers to Start Your Day. She is married, has two children, and resides in Silverdale, Pennsylvania. Pages 8, 76, 152

PAMELA L. MCQUADE has served as a book and magazine editor and has written numerous Christian books. When not writing or reading, she's often quilting or giving belly rubs to her basset hounds. Pages 42, 80, 122, 130, 206

HELEN W. MIDDLEBROOKE is a homemaker, home educator, and the mother of nine. She is a freelance columnist and the author of Lessons for a Supermom. Pages 46, 58, 100

MANDY NYDEGGER lives with her husband, David, in Waco, Texas. She loves Christmas, snow, and the Indianapolis Colts. Pages 12, 32, 52, 98, 150, 170

NICOLE O'DELL, a wife and mother of six, is an accomplished writer of books, devotions, and Bible studies. She has been a Bible study leader and teacher for over fifteen years. Pages 24, 186, 204, 212

MARILEE PARRISH lives in Colorado with her husband, Eric, and young son, Jake. She's a freelance musician and writer who desires to paint a picture of God with her life. Pages 62, 116, 128

RACHAEL PHILLIPS, an award-winning fiction and humor writer, is also the author of four biographies published by Barbour Publishing. Rachael and her husband live in Indiana. Visit her website at www.rachaelwrites.com. Pages 34, 94

RACHEL QUILLIN and her husband, Eric—along with their six children—live on a dairy farm in Ohio. She enjoys gardening, writing, and spending time with her family. Pages 44, 90, 168

JULIE RAYBURN is a public speaker and an area director for Community Bible Study. She lives in Atlanta with her husband, Scott. They have two grown children and one granddaughter. Pages 10, 36, 120, 174, 182

RAMONA RICHARDS is an award-winning author whose books include Secrets of Confidence and A Murder among Friends. Pages 30, 88, 200, 208

KATE E. SCHMELZER graduated from Taylor University in 2008 with a double major in professional writing and counseling and a minor in Christian education. She hopes to be an author, counselor, and missionary. Page 140

LEAH SLAWSON has been married to her husband, Guice, for twenty years. They have two teenagers—a son and daughter. She lives in Montgomery, Alabama. Page 40

TONI SORTOR was a freelance writer and editor in suburban New York. Toni cowrote several Barbour books, including The Word on Life, Prayers and Promises, and Daily Wisdom for Couples. Pages 18, 60, 82, 110, 144, 166, 178, 194, 210

CHRISTAN M. THOMAS is a writer/editor whose work has appeared in magazines and newspapers across Texas and Tennessee. Originally from the Indianapolis area, Christan now resides in Tennessee, with her husband, Brock, and dogs, Tucker and Suzy Q. Pages 14, 54

ANNIE TIPTON is an editor and writer living in small-town Ohio. A former newspaper reporter, she loves her family, friends, sushi, and beach vacations. Pages 66, 176

MARGIE VAWTER is a full-time freelance editor, proofreader, and writer. She lives with her husband in Colorado and enjoys hiking and snowshoeing near their cabin with their two adult children. Page 112

Scripture Index